George Whit White

The Heart and Songs of the Spanish Sierras

George Whit White

The Heart and Songs of the Spanish Sierras

ISBN/EAN: 9783743350083

Manufactured in Europe, USA, Canada, Australia, Japa

Cover: Foto ©Thomas Meinert / pixelio.de

Manufactured and distributed by brebook publishing software (www.brebook.com)

George Whit White

The Heart and Songs of the Spanish Sierras

THE
HEART AND SONGS

OF THE

SPANISH SIERRAS

BY

GEORGE WHIT WHITE

ILLUSTRATED

London
T. FISHER UNWIN
PATERNOSTER SQUARE
MDCCCXCIV

LIST OF ILLUSTRATIONS.

		PAGE
1. THE SEGUIDILLA		*Frontispiece*
2. THE SPIRIT OF THE SIERRAS		13
3. A MOOR OF TANGIERS TO-DAY (*from a photograph*)		31
4. UPS AND DOWNS		121
5. CHILDREN PLAYING		129
6. THE TAUROMACHIAN SCHOOL, SEVILLE		183
7. THE HERO OF THE DAY		193

PREFACE.

THE writer of the following pages went into the Sierras to enjoy himself. While doing so, he bagged a few songs, and felt the heart-beats of a simple, frank, self-respecting race. These, together with the keen sense of enjoyment afforded by the rides, he has endeavoured to describe. Just that, and nothing more.

CRANWELL, SLEAFORD.
1893.

PART I.

MONTAÑAS.

"Es del montañes la gloria
Guardar por antiqua prenda
En una pequeña hacienda
Una grande ejecutoria
Del noble pais la historia
Toda alojeriá embebe,
Y creo, pues se le debe
Al montañes esta maña,
Que es la nobleza de España
Mas cercana de la nieve."[1]
From an undated Spanish Chap Book.

LOOKING back through the telescope of enduring memory upon his wander-

[1] Literal translation :—

"It is the glory of the mountaineer
To preserve, as an ancient heirloom,

ings through the Sierras of Andalucia, the writer sympathises with the sentiments expressed in the native rhyme. It is the mountains that are to-day the peculiar glory of Spain.

And for this reason. At Puerto Santa Maria, for instance (to take a typical Spanish city), the marble *patios*, lofty doorways, and "proud" buildings—no other adjective so fitly describes them—recall vividly the time when the sons of Spain, urged on by zeal for their faith, and the love of gold common to civilised humanity, pushed their fortunes in the

> Though his fortune be small,
> A patent of nobility—
> The history of a noble country.
> His drink honey and pure water.
> Yes, I believe—this, without doubt,
> Is due to the mountaineer—
> That the nobility of Spain
> Dwell nearest to the snow."

New World, despoiled the Incas of Peru, and poured into Spain fabulous sums of gold and silver. That gold and silver, in the course of some three hundred years, has been steadily slipping from her grasp. Grass grows in the streets now, and weeds spring up in the disused balconies. At this day women called *vendedors*, with jewels and ancient gold and silver work concealed about their persons, enter the houses of the rich foreigner, and offer for sale the heirlooms of the Spanish don, the name of the actual seller transpiring never. So the vast treasure of the Incas inevitably filters through at last into the pockets of the race, which, in an incredibly short space of time, by dint of native energy, and not with the aid of Peruvian gold, has caused to spring, as it were from the very bowels of the earth, such cities as Winnipeg and Philadelphia.

Yes, "Ichabod" is written over most of the towns upon the seabord of Spain.

But the everlasting hills remain. There, is now to be found the true glory of Spain. Their souls and bodies fanned by the mountain breeze, untouched by the Incas' gold, the peasantry have preserved intact that noble pride and courteous bearing for which they have been always remarkable, together, moreover, with a touch of nature which makes the whole world kin.

O for a Spanish poet, with the Davidic heart, to fix the Spirit of the Sierras! "Awake up my glory; awake psaltery and harp!"—

> Awake up tinkling, silvery, solitary bells!
> Awake up echoes of solitary human song!
> Bring forth the castanets! Awake up guitar!

THE SPIRIT OF THE SIERRAS.

Well do I remember the day, when, mounted on "Noblé" a sure-footed Barb, in native style, with *alforjas* in which to stow provisions, a revolver, the indispensable **navaja**, a small compass attached to the watch-chain, and a certificate of identity, in case of accident, from the *Ayuntamiento* of Xerez, I started for the Sierras! Heavens! what a glorious sense of untrammelled freedom and independence! I whistled. I ate the air "promise crammed." You cannot feed capons so. From Xerez de la Frontera I had frequently observed, through the glasses, a white spot on the distant mountain. "That is Medina Sidonia," I was told with unconcern by the stay-at-home *Xerezanos*. "Nobody ever goes there."

Medina Sidonia! The name had a

peculiar fascination for me. Was not the Spanish Armada, that magnificent and proud attempt to convert our tight little island, unwillingly commanded by the Duke of that name? How many to-day in busy Europe ever had anything to do with the place, or know anything whatever about it? There it lay over there, nestling in the mountain, "amid a busy world alone." Surely it must be, of very necessity, a self-contained, pastoral city! And now my curiosity was to be gratified. Passing over the winding Guadalete, I struck the track alone for the wild Sierras!

But if the air, as I have said, goes some way—indeed a long way—towards satisfying the appetite, Sunny Spain is a thirsty land. I began to be athirst, and to look out for a well

—yes, believe me, nothing less than a well! At length came to one. Two Andalucians, on beautiful horses, with quaint saddles, and box-stirrups painted green, in charge of a drove of fine springy, long-pasterned colts, and two goatherds, all evidently from Medina, approached at the same time from the opposite direction. With graceful courtesy to the stranger, one of the goatherds drew me up a bucket of water. I dismounted, and drank from the bucket a deep, long draught, like an ox. This much amused the Andalucians, who have a saying, which I only now appreciated to the full, "*Aqua como buey, vino como rey*"—"Drink water like an ox, wine like a king." I then brought out from the recesses of the *alforja* my ham, hard-boiled eggs and *navaja*, and, like a true

Andaluz, said, "*Guste Vds comer?*"—
"Will your Graces be pleased to dine?" A
kinship was immediately established with
the *Inglez*. Their hearts were very easily
won. Strange to say, Noblé did not
care for the water, but contented himself
with playing with it, and then, with
cocked ears, took an immense interest
in his brethren as they surrounded the
trough and drank their fill. He couldn't
attend to anything else. When, with a
"*Vaya Vd. con Dios*," the Andalucians
pursued their way with their charges,
Noblé was also so far satisfied with the
stock he had taken of the strangers of
his kind that he would doubtless have
kicked up his heels and been after them
if I hadn't held him tight.

Up and off again through the path or
no path, past immense herds of claret-

coloured pigs in charge of boys—dark skinned little rascals. One of them, I noticed, with a face like a picture of Murillo's, was lying down reading a book! I wish I had asked his Grace to let me see what he was reading, but I could not have done so without being rude. He was quite absorbed in it. There were also flocks of what appeared to be very profitable fine goats—the Sierras are the paradise of goats—and Merino sheep. Now and again there crossed the path a golden oriole, honey buzzard, or butcher-bird (the latter more like a dainty little gentleman than a butcher, by the way), but no singing birds to compete with the goatherd as, clad in sheepskin, but with the instinct and manners of a gentleman, he tends his tinkling flock and, under his native sky, far from railways and the strife of tongues, gives forth his gentle human heart in solitary improvised song :—

>Amantito, **Amantito,**
>Amante, Amante,
>Las pestañas me estorban
>Para mirarte.

>(Little sweetheart, little sweetheart,
>My love, my love,
>Thine eyelashes are in the way
>Of my gazing on thee.)

>¡ (Qué largas las horas son
>En el reloj del afan,
>Y qué poco á poco dan
>Alivio á mi corazon !

>(How long are the hours
>Of the clock of anxiety!
>How little, little relief
>Do they give my heart !)

>Triste esta mi corazon
>Y no sabe lo que tiene ! . . .
>Que está muy léjos de aqui
>El que consolarlo puede.

(Sad is my heart
And I know not what ails it ! . . .
Somebody is far from hence
Who could comfort it.)

Los ojos de mi morena
Ie paracen a mis males,
Grandes como mis fatigas,
Meros como mis pesares.

(The eyes of my brown bread
Appear like unto my sorrows.
They are great—like my toils,
Black—like my griefs.)

En la soledad del campo
Me puse á llorar mis penas
Y fueron tantos mis llantos
Que florecieron las yervas.

(In the solitude of the field
I sat me down and my trials bemoaned.
So copious were my tears
That the flowers bloomed.)[1]

---

[1] This conceit is very pretty when it is remembered that in this sun-baked land the wild flowers spring up as if by magic after the copious showers. They are so abundant at times that it seems a pity to ride over them.

Estrellas del alto cielo,
Bajad y firmad por mi :
Que cumpliré la palabra
Que al que está ausente le di.

(Stars of the high heavens
Descend and certify for me,
That I will fulfil the vow
Made to my absent love.)

Las estrellitas di cielo
Cada cual tiene su nombre ;
La mia se llama Rita,
Le llamo y no me responde !

(Little stars of heaven,
Each one has its name ;
Mine is named Rita ;
I call—yet it does not reply !)

Una porcion de Civiles
Han salido de Moron
En busca de unos ladrones ;
Mi niña, tus ojos son.

(A band of Civil Guards
Have set out from Moron
In pursuit of robbers ;
The robbers were your eyes, girl !)

Tus ojos son ladrones
Que roban y hurtan,
Tus pestañas el monte
Donde se ocultan.

(Thine eyes are robbers
That rob and steal,
Thine eyelashes the wood
That hides them.)

Te quiero mas que el dinero,
Mas que á mi padre y mi madre,
Y si no fuese pecado
Mas que a la Virgen del Carmen.

(I love thee more than money,
More than father and mother,
And, were it no sin,
More than the Virgin of Carmel.)

Me llamen el celoso,
A mi ! qué pena !
Soy labrador y quiéro
Guardar mi hacienda.

(They call me the jealous one,
Ah me ! what a shame !
I am a cultivator and only want
To keep trespassers off my farm.)[1]

---

[1] It should be remarked that the farms in Andalucia are not laid out and hedged in as in England,

Con la luz te comparo,
¡ Mira qué dicha !
Sin la luz no se puede
Celebrar misa.[1]

(With the light I compare thee,
Ah! what good fortune!
Without light they cannot
Celebrate mass.)

Compadécete de mi,
Que tienes el corazon
Mas duro que las columnas
Del templo de Salomon.

(Take pity on me!
Ah! thy heart is harder
Than the columns
Of Solomon's Temple.)

---

and one may very well trespass upon them without being aware of it. As related later on, I did this once. A voice, proceeding from a gesticulating figure in the far distance, greeted my ears. I gesticulated back to the jealous one that I was an unwitting trespasser and had hopes some day of getting clear of his property.

[1] The rubric for the mass in the Spanish Church enjoins that mass may not be celebrated without at least two lights.

Dos estrellas se han perdido
Y en el cielo no parecen,
En tu casa se han metido
Y en tu cara resplandecen.

(Two stars have been lost
And appear not in the heavens,
They are lodged in thy house
And in thy countenance shine.)

Sin duda que tu padre
Fué confitero,
Y te hizo los labios
De caramelo.

(Without doubt
Your father was a *confitero*
And moistened thy lips
With caramel.)

Suddenly Medina Sidonia, ever gleaming white, comes into view, but is lost again and again behind the hills, like a *señorita* coquetting with her fan. Even when ascending the very steep and rocky ascent to the city it disappears again—seems to have vanished into space. Emerged close upon it at last.

It happened to be the last day of the fair, as I afterwards learnt. From silence and solitude I came suddenly, startlingly, upon throbbing, pulsating human life. It was half-past seven. I turned for one brief moment to bid farewell to the unclouded sun, setting now, in the brown, gold, and purple glory peculiar to the Spanish atmosphere.

.   .   .   .   .

There fled swiftly past me from the city, methought distraught and proud, the spectral form of a Moorish knight on a Barb like the noble animal on which I sat, disappeared quickly down the steep descent, then reappeared again and again, as he pursued his solitary way along the winding path that I had just traversed—his lance glittering in the advancing moonlight—Zayde! Zayde!! Zayde!!!—the lessening echoes came back, until finally lost in the stillness of the night.

.   .   .   .   .

It was but a momentary vision of an episode in that most romantic chapter of the history of Spain, the Moorish occupation.

"SALE LA ESTRELLA DE VENUS."

Now comes forth the Star of Venus,
The sun t'advancing night in dying glory yields,
A darkening mantle, slowly, surely
Is winding round the Earth's green fields.
See, see, yon Moor, in hot haste speeding
Through Sidonia's open gate!
Dark his brow, and proud his bearing,
Yet his heart is desolate.
On by the winding Guadalete,
By the sunny plains of Xeréz,
Hard by the port of famous name,[1]

---
[1] Puerto Santa Maria—*la Santisima y Purisima.*

He hastens ever, on his lonely way;
Desperate, forlorn, on, on he travels.
Though of noble lineage comes he,
His faithless fair has falsely left him,
Taunting him with poverty.
Upon a Moor, base, **uncomely**,
Though wealthy and **in high** command,
—Of yon Torre [1] Warden, of Seville Alcalde—
To-night she bestows her perjured hand.
Of a wrong so **hard** he murmurs;
"Zayde!" . . . Echo to his heart adds fuel,
Echoing back his piteous cry.
"Zayde! Zayde!!" . . . **far more cruel**
Than the ship-destroying **waves!**
Colder, more inexorable far
Than yon dark and lonesome caves!
"How canst thou, cruel **one**, forget **me?**
Wilt thou that my only jewels
Should other hands adorn?
Canst thou entwine thy youthful **tendrils**
Around an old and blasted tree,
Leaving mine all bared **and** fruitless,
Leaves all scattered—bared by thee?
He, thy choice, **is poor,** though **wealthy,**
He thou leavest rich, though poor,
Than rich blood, and wealth of **spirit**

---

[1] Probably the *Torre de la Estrella* (The Tower of the Star), the ruins of which still exist near Medina Sidonia. **See also** remarks on the City Blazonry later on.

Mere bags of dross dost value more?
How canst thou thy Gazul abandon
—Six sweet years of love, now flown—
To give thine hand to Albenzayde
Till but yesterday unknown?
Allah! Allah! . . . grant he may
Thee hate, abhor—thou him adore.
May jealousy and absence gnaw thee,
Sweet sleep ne'er close thine eyelids more,
No longed-for rest by day restore thee.
May he give thy due to others.
Mayst thou at Tournament despised be;
At *Zambra*[1] no more seen thy colours;
Nay, mayst thou with his cipher see
Another maiden's name entwined;
May he give to her his captives,
Yet be to thee—in mockery—kind.
May thy "husband," dead, be borne
From battle with the Christian foe
Ere he enfold thee or enjoy thee.
May justice shower on thee this heritage of woe!
But, ah! shouldst thou indeed abhor him,
For countless ages be he thine!
No greater malediction
Could wit of devil or man divine."

. . . .

See now by light of yonder moon, on, on he spurs,
Straight for Xeréz, to the Palace—Hark, the voices!
Hark, the gay song! See, hither, thither,

---

[1] A Moorish feast.

Moving, turbaned Moors, with lighted torches!
Through this unheeding throng in knightly saddle hies
    he,
Apparently his tardy courtesies to pay.
. . . Ah ! a bloody lance has pierced
Albenzayde's eager breast !
Confusion in the plaza ! Oh, what horror and dismay !
Through all, with reeking sword, the Moor, avengéd,
Back to Medina takes his way.

But to return to present living realities. The *alameda* outside the city walls was thronged with young men and maidens, old men and children. There was a distinct hum, in the glorious eventide, of human voices, unmingled with any other sound — unmistakably as of people enjoying the joy of existence. After complete solitude, the sudden effect upon the mind was singularly thrilling. Evidently here was no everlasting walk up and down, or sitting in chairs upon the *pasao*, as

A MOOR OF TANGIERS TO-DAY.
(*From a Photograph*).

in more sophisticated cities, but life, brisk movement, and love-making pure and simple. The very movement of the girls' fans said that these people did not care much how the rest of the world wagged. They evidently got on very well without the very latest news. And as for telegrams, the only telegrams they looked anxiously for were those shot by their *novias*.

Gentle reader and critic, if you smell out heresy in the above sentence I must plead for just one word of explanation, if not of justification, before being consigned to the flames. This is a history of personal impressions jotted down from a diary. It may explain matters, then, if I confess that whenever I read a daily paper I prefer that of the day before yesterday—fact! There is something barbarous in eating freshly-killed meat, almost quivering with life. So, it seems to me, is it with quite fresh news. Let both hang a little; they will both be more digestible.

Put up at a *posada*—"*Del Vista Hermosa.*" Sometimes the *posadas*, and all the vineyards I had hitherto seen, had been dedicated to "*Nuestra Señora*" de *Rosario*, "*del Soledad,*" and so on, so that I could not help making a note of this sign as falling in with my impression of the pastoral character of this city, which also has a quotation from the Psalms of David inscribed upon her blazonry! "Dominus salvavit me: Ego autem ad Deum clamavi."

A quotation from the Psalms, inscribed upon city blazonry, or for the matter of that upon any blazonry, is, I have reason to believe, quite unique in the history of heraldry. Strangely enough also the *coplas* sung in the neighbourhood sometimes allude, as will have been seen in the examples given, to Solomon's Temple, King Saul, and King David. This is interesting, when it is observed that these people derive their origin from Tyre and Sidon in Northern Palestine.

I also noticed upon the city arms the representation of a tower—*donjoned, watch-towered,* and *turretted*—surmounted with a star of silver. This would probably be the *Torre de la Estrella* referred to in the Moorish ballad given above.

After giving Noblé a feed of barley and straw, rubbing him down, locking up saddle, bridle, and *alforjas* in the bedroom, and doing rigid justice to a dinner of fried eggs, I strolled out gaily to see the fun of the fair. In the *Calle San Juan* were booths at which sweets and cheap toys were being sold, much in the same way as at an English fair. In the *Plazuela de Crux* were numbers of little tables set out with every imaginable contrivance for gambling, of an innocent sort, around which the youths and young men of the town clustered, and played with their *reals*. A young, good-looking priest was strolling about among them. He wasn't scowling. Further on, in the *Plaza de la Constitucion*, I found that the people had come in with nightfall from the outside *alameda* and were now promenading under Chinese lanterns. What chiefly attracted my attention was the walk and carriage of the girls and women. It was almost a revelation.

They never walk arm-in-arm, nor, I am informed, do they lace too tightly. Perhaps that has something to do with it.

After enjoying the life and movement of the fair for some time, I returned to the *posada*, welcomed with a neigh by Noblé. Then, making up his bed, and giving him another feed of barley and straw, turned in myself. Awoke during the night and looked out through the *réja*. There passed by, in the flesh, in the moonlight, a *sereno* with halbert and lantern, his cry, in measured cadence:—

A · ve, Ma · ria, pu · ri · si · ma.

being now the only sound that broke the stillness of the night-watches.

Next morning, guided by the sign of

the "Helmet of Mambrino," I entered a *barbero's* and had an exquisite shave. That operation completed, to the accompaniment of a talk about Don Quixote's adventure with the barber, at which our friend was so much amused that I thought he would cut me, I dried my face and had a chat with an intelligent young agriculturalist in the shop. "Medina," said he with much gusto, "is a fine place—much better than any other city in the province. Cadiz is fine, but it is always the *pasao*, nothing but the *pasao*, whereas here is the *campo* and game," pointing to a decoy partridge [1] hanging up in the shop. Every one seemed to possess one of these decoy

---

[1] "Like as a partridge taken (and kept) in a cage, so is the heart of the proud; and like as a spy watcheth he for thy fall."—ECCLESIASTICUS xi. 30.

birds. He was just the sort of young fellow, I thought, to be the hero of the following rollicking *Ventana* song:—

RECLAMO.

Tu 'eres palomita blanca
y yo palomito azul,
juntaremos los piquitos
y haremos cu—cu—bru—cu.

I.

Lola, sal a la Ventana,
que sin tus ojos no hay luz,
y está en tenieblas la calle
y tengo mucha inquietud,
porque tan solo y á oscuras
pudiera comerme el bú.
Ya sé, Lola, que tu madre
dice que soy un Gandul,
y que me paso la vida
jugando al cané y al mús;
pero no debes hacer
caso de la vieja tú.
Piensa, Lola, en que tu Pepe
es de amantes el non plus,
que te quiere, y te requiere,
y te querrá doble aún,
con un corazon más grande
que de aquí á Calatayud.

Con que sal á la ventana,
perla del reino Andaluz,
que eres palomita blanca
y yo palomito azul;
sal, y á través de la reja,
ya que en la calle no hay luz,
juntaremos los piquitos
y haremos cu—cu—bru—cu.

II.

¿ No sales, Lola? Sin duda
No conoces mi inquietud
cuando no abres la ventana!
¡ Por vida del Rey Saul !
¿ Será quizá que á tu padre,
que es un pedazo de atun,
—y dispénsame el requiebro—
se le ha puesto en el testuz
que te ausentes y no salgas?
Dile que no haga el mambrú,
que lo que yo estoy haciendo
él lo hizo en su juventud ;
que no pretendo ser cura
ni quieres ser monja tú ;
que ya para bien de todos
se abolió la esclavitud ;
que si casada has de ser
debes jugar el albur ;
que prohibírtelo sería
en él una ingratitud ;

que eres palomita blanca
y yo palomito azul;
que queremos arrularnos,
ya que en la calle no hay luz,
y que bajito, bajito,
haremos cu—cu—bru—cu.

III.

¡ Lola, muchacha ! ¿ no sales ?
¡ Por vida de Belcebú
que me va cansando, Lola,
mi pacífica actitud !
Si es que mi amoroso afan
no te importa un altramuz,
ó que tu padre y tu madre,
obrando de mancomun,
no quieren salgas á verme,
dilo y emigro al Peru.
Mas ¿ qué es esto?   La ventana
siento abrir. . . . ¡ Lola !
                        —¡ Gandul,
deja tranquila á la chica,
ó por vida de Esaú
que te rompo las costillas !
¿ Has entendido ?
                    ¡ Jesús !
¡ Es su padre !
                —Si, su padre,
que va á reventarle aún
si no te quitas de en medio.

¡ Pues no tengo poca cruz
contigo ! Toda la noche
estás rurrun que rurrun,
sin dejar dormér á nadie.
—Pues si busca usté quietud
deje salír á la Lola.
—Vete de la reja tú.
—¿ **Irme yo** ? ¡ No, señor ; **cá** !
no me mueve **ni un** obús.
Ella es palomita blanca
y yo palomito azul.
—Pues como tome una **tranca**
te daré el cu—cu—bru—cu.

THE DECOY BIRD.

> Thou shalt be a white dove
> And I a blue,
> We'll join our little beaks
> And cry Cu—cu—rru—cu.

I.

Lola ! Come to the window.
There's no light without thine **eyes**
And the street in darkness lies.
I'm so restless,
It's so lonely and **dark**—
A Bogey might eat me.
Your mother, Lola, I know well,
Calls me a *Gandul*,
Says I spend my life
Playing at *cané* and *el mus*.

But don't heed the old woman;
Remember Lola that your Pepe
Is of lovers the *non plus*,
That he loves you, and loves you,
And loves you, with a heart
As wide as from here to *Calatayud*.
Then come to the window,
Pearl of the kingdom of *Andaluz*,
You shall be a white dove
And I a blue ;
Come, love, then to the grating—
There is no light in the street—
We will join our little beaks
And cry *Cu—cu—Bru—cu.*

II.

Won't you appear, Lola?
You cannot know how my heart trembles,
Or sure you would come to the window !
By the life of King Saul !
Perhaps your father,
Who is a lump of tunny fish—
Excuse the endearing expression—
Has taken it into his noddle
That you absent yourself,
And that's why you don't appear !
Tell him not to play the *Mambru*
For what I am now doing
He did in his youth ;
That I am not ambitious to be a curé,

And you don't want to be a nun,
That for the good of all
Slavery is abolished.
That if married you are to be
You should play at *Albur;*
That to forbid it thee
Were base ingratitude ;
That you will be a white dove
And I a blue,
That we wish to bill and coo,
—There is no light in the street—
And softly, softly,
Cry *Cu—cu—Bru—cu.*

III.

Lola, *Muchacha!*[1] Won't you come ?
By the life of Beelzebub
I am getting weary, Lola,
Of this lonely state.
If my anxiety of heart
Doesn't matter an *altramuz* to you,
Or if your father and mother both
With one consent
Won't let you come out to see me,
Say so—and I'm off for Peru !

---

[1] It is best not to translate this word. The essence of the fun is that he is becoming impatient, and so, in contrast to "the pearl of the kingdom of Audaluz," he now simply calls her *muchacha*, the ordinary word for a girl.

But stay—What's that?
. . . The window . . . I feel it opens. . . .
Lola !
  —*Gandul !*
Leave the girl alone,
Or, by the life of Esau !
I'll break your ribs.
Dost understand?
                    Jesu!
It's her father !
            —Yes, her father.
Who's going to smash you up
If you don't get out of this.
It's no small cross I have to bear,
With you all night long
Whispering and calling
Letting no one sleep.
Well, if you want quiet
Let Lola come forth !
—Get away from the grating, will you !
I go away? No, Señor, not I.
An *obus* shall not move me.
For she is a white dove
And I a blue.
—Wait till I get a stick
  I'll give you the *Cu—cu—Bru—cu.*

The mule trappings and bells are the most interesting things sold at the fair. The latter are of rude construction but very sweet sound, and the peasantry try the different tones with a critical ear before buying. The bells keep the mules in heart, they say. And this certainly is the case. The mule is often spoken of as obstinate, but without sufficient reason, I think. The fine Spanish animals—the *garañon*, or product of the mare and the ass, being the finest—seemed to me quite remarkably patient, docile, and willing. The soothing tinkle tinkle of the bells no doubt has something to do with it. Truly animals, as well as races of men, are often given a bad name without deserving it. Purchased a set of bells, together with a *borracha*, as mementos of my visit. Then up and off for *Vejer*.

Upon the outskirts I came upon two peasant girls dancing. It was not for show. There were only an elderly woman (probably the mother), an elderly peasant, and a little child near, and they were taking no notice. It was the spontaneous, free, uncorsetted expression of the growing, warm, young human heart, there being no accompaniment save the music of their own heartstrings, set in motion, like those of an Æolian harp, by the air of their native Sierras. The whole body danced: the arms, raised with natural grace, eyes, mouth, bosom, waist, and legs—the latter not more than other parts of body and soul. As to any mere vulgar exhibition of limbs, it could not enter the imagination even. Indeed, the movements of these daughters of the South expressed upon God's earth, of which they were the fairest ornaments, the very poetry of motion, even as does the flight of the swallow in the air.

Upon my passing near, there was no prudery or shamefacedness. They did not stop. Why should they? The *Señor Caballero* was as welcome to sip of their joy as he would have been to share the family *olla podrida* under their father's roof. Ah me! he may be sad, like the knight of the sorrowful figure, but he is not churlish. He will not say—no, that he won't!—

> "I ne'er saw nectar on a lip
> But where my own did hope to sip."

Nay, the pretty native *copla* rather expressed his feelings:—

> "Esos dos que están bailando
> ¡ Qué parejitós que son !
> Si yo fuese Padre Cura,
> Les daba la bendicion."

("Those two that are dancing
What a little pair they are!
If I were the Father Curé
I would give them the benediction.")

I have said that the mother was near. The unreserved sympathy in matters of the heart between mother and daughters, who are so full of love, from the crown of the head to the sole of the foot, that a stray beam could no more be prevented from lighting upon a passing *caballero*, than the sun's rays could be shut out by transparent glass, finds expression in the following dialogue between a mother and her daughter:—

CRECERÉ Y DÁRSELOS HE.

Daughter.

To yonder *caballero*, mother,
I send three kisses all my own,
Which he shall have when I am grown.
  ('Twas the first offering of virgin youth.)

To flatter only with my love, O mother mine,
Were not a virtue, but a crime.
Should he ere to claim his due pass by,
Three kisses I will not deny,
Three kisses, mother, all my own,
Which he shall have when I am grown.

Mother.

Nay, 'twere no sin, child,
Such vows as these to rend.
Abhor, detest them,
Cast them from thee.
'Twere not for thee *such* beads to tell
Who'rt pledged to serve Our Lady
In convent cell.

Daughter.

Nay, he shall have them when I'm grown,
For, mother, you've often taught me
That who held good would be
At any time for good or ill,
His word, though he die, must needs fulfil.
Then die I'd rather than my word disown,
Nay! he shall have them, mother, when I'm grown.

Mother.

Sweet daughter mine!
No judge on high,
A rash promise broken,
At thy tender age,
Would "guilty" decry.

Daughter.

Nay, he must have them, mother—why?
I cannot perjured be, though I should die;
    For to cavalier so gentle,
    God forbid such scorn be shown.
Then he must have them, mother, when I'm grown.

The approach to Vejer from Medina is very beautiful. The town is in the most striking situation I had yet seen: comes into view—gleaming white as ever in this smokeless land—upon the top of a precipitous rocky mountain, the sides of which are covered with snapdragon and a perfect wealth of sedums and saxafrages. At the base stretches a flat valley, very fertile, a river winding through with picturesque bridges that would be the delight of an artist. Another precipitous, green-covered, solitary mountain rises to the left; a ravine, in serpentine continuation of the valley, passing between. To the right a still higher mountain, while all around the valley swells the bosom of Mother Earth in lines of perfect beauty. In the background the blue Sierras, with a bloom upon them like the bloom upon a ripe plum.

At the base of the steep and winding ascent to the city the *consumos* were standing about as usual, seeking whom they might devour. They let me pass without question, but, apparently, afterwards changed their mind (thinking perhaps that my *alforjas* looked as if they contained *something*) and called after me with the universal Spanish hiss, equivalent to our "Hie!" I was, however, afflicted with sudden deafness, and pushed on. It was like walking up the side of a house. The fact is, in

Spain, it is a solemn duty to "do" the *consumos*; and I never heard of anybody sending conscience-money to the Exchequer. Ever and anon, to prolong the sense of enjoyment, I stopped and turned to take in and assimilate the varying scene; for is not a thing of beauty, so assimilated, "a joy for ever"?

> "Its loveliness increases; it will never
> Pass into nothingness."

While so standing, at one point, I was overtaken by an Andaluz on a fine black horse. He was evidently accustomed to seeing Englishmen, admired Noblé, the make of bridle, saddle, &c., and wished to conduct me into the town, I believe honestly—he had an honest face. As, however, it is prudent, when alone in these Sierras, to be wary, and chary of giving information about one's movements, I politely declined, and wished him adieu with a "*Vaya Vd. con Dios.*"

Upon entering the town, his manner was explained. The English were evidently known and, what is more, liked. Inquired of a donkey-boy the way to a *posada*. He told me. Some men, however, who had been watching my approach from above, called out to him, "*Este un Inglez*," implying that he might have done something more. It was amusing to see how the boy incontinently left his string of donkeys all untended and acted as my guide to the *posada*. Here I was welcomed as if I had been a prince, although the prince's fare was to consist only of the inevitable fried eggs. And, *mirabile dictu!* had they not a piece of soap? For once I let the boy unsaddle Noblé, and observed that he was very careful to do everything exactly as he was told. The fact is that English officers from Gibraltar are accustomed to come here for bustard shooting in the *lagune* some three miles off. The boy showed me round the town with much importance. What became of his donkeys all the while did not trouble him a bit. He would find them, no doubt, *mañana*.

Like all these mountain *pueblos* the interior was disappointing. It reminded me a little of Tangiers. Upon returning to the *posada*, before turning in, I entered a room where, in darkness, the mistress, cook, and servant were seated round a *brasero*. Sat down with them to finish my cigar and have a chat. While talking, it struck me after a time that my audience was very attentive. Upon closer observation, however, found that the cook and servant were fast asleep. The effect was soporific. The cigar dropped from my grasp, and, overcome by the spirit of the place, I nearly fell into the *brasero*. So raising my arms in yawning benediction over the sleepers, I vanished to my own room to take my rest in the ordinary posture.

In the morning departure was delayed by the rain. The mistress entered my room without ceremony, accompanied by her daughter, powdered—Spanish women use a great deal of powder. She had come to introduce her. Spanish mothers are always delighted if you take notice of their daughters, and one need make no bones about admiring their beauty. It is the custom to transparently look at them in the street and say, "Olé! Olé!" as they pass. A girl, when properly got up for the purpose, is disappointed if she returns from her walk and has not been noticed. It need not be said that she is invariably accompanied by her *duenna*. There happened to be a certificate of merit from a school hanging up in the room. I asked if it was hers. It was. She was very pleased, and fetched her school-books, a geography, history, &c., arranged in the form of question and answer. I asked her some questions. She blushed, and either could not or was too nervous to answer. Well, I am sure I should not be certain of being able to answer questions from the school-books of my childhood. There was something affected, however, about this interview, and it failed to leave a favourable impression.

It having ceased to rain about eleven o'clock, I descended to saddle Noblé. The whole establishment stood round at a respectful distance to watch the operation. I could see it was expected that I should be impatient, so I hustled my town boy of the day before, who had turned up again, to get something with which to pick out the horse's feet. He brought me a stick which broke (there happened to be a large flint in the hoof); I stormed. He then brought a ridiculous little knife. Looking as if I were going to demolish him, I dropped Noblé's leg and looked round myself for what I wanted. Being mounted and ready to depart, I gave them a tip all round, *à l'Anglaise*, and off for Chiclana.

The fact is, that constant contact with Englishmen — although, as they had been, doubtless, for the most part, gentlemen, it had not bred either contempt or dislike—had spoiled these people. In their simplicity they are inveterate imitators, and in proportion as they imitate the foreigner, especially the *Inglez*, their charm is gone for ever. In towns such as Xerez this is very apparent. Take women's head-dress, for instance. It has been said (not by me) that women are more careful than men to adorn the *outside* of the head. Cock birds of paradise, kittiwakes, and other beautiful things are ruthlessly slaughtered for the purpose. Among birds, however, nature seems to have lavished outside ornaments upon the *male*. The single bright flower which Spanish women place in the hair, and their manner of arranging the hair and head-covering are singularly graceful and natural. Many of them, however, will persist in imitating the *Inglez*, and adopting the cosmopolitan hat—generally, I have observed, of the broad brimmed variety, and plentifully adorned. I wish they wouldn't do so. Gallantry forbids me to say more.

Went out of my way a little to visit Conil, a primitive fishing *pueblo* on the coast. Evidently an Englishman was much more of a *rara avis* here. Pulled up in front of the Franciscan Convent de la Victoria. Introducing myself with a cigar to a *Guardia Civile* standing by, he told me something about the place. The house adjoining the convent and in front of which we were standing was the *alcaldia*. He asked if I should like to see the secretary. Having no affairs of state on hand I did not do so. The tower below us facing the sea was the *Torre de Guzman*, one of those Moorish towers so common in Andalucia. The coloured markings on this one, I observed, were still extant. While we were chatting, Noblé had been nibbling at the tufts of grass growing out of the stone seats. His bridle caught in one of the iron supports and dragged it from the socket, pulling away stones and mortar with it. It did not matter. "It can be mended *mañana*," said my friend. Query! All the town struck me as being in this expectant state. The crumbling walls will be restored *mañana*. Truly, "To-morrow, and to-morrow, and to-morrow creeps on its petty pace from day to day, to the last syllable of recorded time." Said "*Buenos tarde*" to the *Guardia*, and made for a *venta*. Bought a bundle of clover on the way, which Noblé enjoyed at the door, while his master, bringing out ham and bread from the *alforja* and calling for a *caña* of *manzanilla*, also enjoyed his regal repast, then lighted a cigarette and surveyed the faces of the shoeless fisher-boys and girls—nice expressions—who had clustered round to gaze at the *caballero*. Called one very pretty brown child and asked if she liked *confiteria*. She was very shy, but eventually avowed the soft impeachment.

Up and off once more for Chiclana,

San Fernando, Cadiz, and home. Passing through Chiclana I bought a paper —the "*Toreo*"—of a blindman. They have, I was told, the monopoly of selling certain papers, and also have the privilege of listening to hear the winning numbers at the national lotteries. The numbers so heard are published before the certified official list. The poor fellow did not fail to say "*Vaya Vd. con Dios*" on leaving the unseen purchaser. I could not help thinking, as he groped his way on calling out his papers, how applicable the salutation was to himself. Blindness seems to be rather common. I remember that after leaving Medina Sidonia, of the very few people I met three wore large goggles, apparently suffering from ophthalmia.

San Fernando might well be called

Salt Lake City. The road thereto lies through flat, marshy land, cut out into salt pans, and on either side everywhere are huge pyramids of salt, looking like the tents of an army in the field. I remembered Lot's wife.

Passed through the town and made for Cadiz along the sea-shore. Fine firm sand. The coast reminded me very much of the coast of Suffolk near Southwold and Walberswick, and, sure enough, it is also a breeding ground of the same tern I have seen there. They seem to delight in a low shore where there are tufts of stunted grass above a line of beach. Saw also many sandpipers, just as in Suffolk. Both of us being somewhat travel-stained, I thought Noblé might like a bath. When he quite understood that the advancing little waves (the sea was now in one of her gentle moods) were not going to swallow him up, he enjoyed it very much. A *consumo* fellow, gun in hand, stood watching the performance from the road above. He evidently came to the conclusion that I was trying to evade the Customs by going to sea on horseback, and ran straight down to the shore with long strides to prevent my doing so—by catching hold of Noblé's tail, I imagine. He, however, was courteous enough, simply felt my *alforjas*, and took my word for it that I had nothing excisable about me. I must say that I should not think of evading these legal dues—when a fellow has a gun !

Ah ! fair, white, marble Cadiz ! As I sat in one of the embrasures of the ramparts to the west of the city—a man peacefully fishing with a rod beneath, the *feluccas* and *misticos* skimming like sea-birds the blue waters of the bay, on the other side of which rose fair Gades, white as white could be (for there is no smoke to blacken it), backed by the Sierra de Ronda—I acknowledged in my heart what a beautiful city it was. As I then rose and wandered through her narrow, cool streets, beheld the lofty white houses, lofty marble doorways, patios, and high balconies—not too high (they could not be that) for the lightning glance of her women to pierce through the heart of many a passer-by below—and sat down at length by the plashing fountain in the Plaza de Minha, I was fairly impressed with the pride of the Spaniard of bygone days, and also felt how well it may be, as reported, that Venus reigns here and exacts full homage to her charms. I seemed to see, too, through the near episode of the Moorish occupation, distinctly, Rome. It was the Romans who first built the city of marble, and under the sway of Rome she became extremely wealthy, having the monopoly for the supply of salt fish to the Empire City.

As, from its position, Cadiz is a city seldom visited on horseback, I found that the only place where I could put up Noblé was at the *posada* at the back of the town, then crowded with *arrieros*. Not quite liking the idea of leaving him and all my belongings there for the night, I resolved to sleep on the spot. The bedroom and bed right above the open stables (containing now between three hundred and four hundred donkeys and mules) were quite clean and comfortable, but oh! gentle reader, have you ever tried to sleep with a Jack donkey braying right into your ear, not only once or twice, but every minute or so? As I could not afford to lose a night's rest, I rose, dressed, and, quietly locking the room door and putting the key in my pocket, stole out unobserved and took a bed at the Hotel de Paris in the *Calle San Francisco.* It was surrounded with a mosquito curtain. As I lay down I could hear a service being rendered in an adjoining church, the deep voice of the solo singer and the notes of the grand piano, together with a faint smell of incense being borne in at the open window. It was so different to the surrounding sounds at the *posada* just before that in a half-dreamy, not unpleasing, contemplation of the varying aspects of human life, I dropped off to sleep.

Found all right at the *posada* next morning. Mounted and off for the last stage home. Took the shore again as far as San Fernando; thence to Puerto Real. Then, instead of striking the regular road for Puerto Santa Maria, and thence to Xerez, I thought I would try a short cut. After some time entered a sweet-smelling pine wood, where there were abundance of flowers, especially, I noticed, of the white cistus kind. Upon emerging from this wood, I apparently took the wrong track, entered another wood, and went on and on, gradually losing all trace of a pathway. I knew, however, that there are no large forests in this country, and that if I pushed on I must soon emerge into the open. The wood became denser and denser—in fact almost impassable. Emerged, however, at length, and saw by the broad light of day a man tending cattle a short distance off. He pointed out the direction of Xerez. Thought I would make for it as the crow flies. More easily said than done. Many obstacles presented themselves, such as sudden, precipitous breaks in the hills, vast cultivated fields, necessitating many annoying detours. On these extensive rolling *haciendas*, without dividing hedge or ditch, the fallow runs so insensibly into the cultivated lands that I did not realise, until I heard a voice shouting at me, that for some time I had been riding over somebody's *garbanzos*. I have heard of a boy who, when caught in an orchard and asked where he was going, said, very meekly, " Back again." I thought it best, however, to keep straight on, and eventually got out, as luck would have it, in the right direction. After crossing the next hill, what I rightly took to be the *Cartuja* appeared in sight. Patting my good old servant, Noblé, on the neck, we soon covered the distance between us at a gallop. Once more crossing the *Cartuja* bridge, I dismounted at a spring a little way beyond the convent, drank a deep, long draught of the delicious water direct from the spring, in the waning light—so beautiful, the faint purple, golden brown of the sunset being reflected in the sparkling stream—let Noblé have a drink, washed his legs and rubbed him down, then up and off for Xerez, where the *Caballero Inglez* and steed arrived at 8.30 p.m., without a scratch, after the most delightful holiday he had ever had.

PART II.

> "If there's a hole in a' your coats,
> Ye need na tent it;
> A chiel's amang ye, taking notes,
> But he'll na prent it."
> *Pace* ROBERT BURNS.

ANOTHER more extended ride was to the Serrania of Ronda. Equipment this time at starting a *paté de foie gras!* flask of brandy, a bottle of *Vino de Xerez* (sherry), the invaluable tea, Cockle's pills, chlorodyne, flea powder, a revolver, compass, and map of the province. The road to Arcos de la Frontera, the first stage, is a *carretera de 1º orden*, very well made and preserved. Indeed I have observed that the roads in this country are either very good or execrable. At certain distances apart there are *Casillas de Peones Camineros*, where men with a uniform with red facings permanently reside, their duty being to keep the road in order. Many of them, I noticed, carried a gun. This road runs through the Caulena valley, rich in wild flowers and bulbs. Passing the ruins of the Castle of Malgarejo, now tenanted by great numbers of blue jays, Arcos comes into view, the situation being quite remarkable. The city is built upon a bold spur of the mountain which runs out into the valley, coming right up to the edge of a broken precipice. It looks as if some day it must come down with a crash. Pushed on for El Bosque.

The way to El Bosque lies for the greater part through large cork woods. It is curious to observe how the bark of the living trees is covered with lichen, fungi, ferns, and saxafrages; also the fantastic, weird shapes assumed by many of the branches. It is like riding through the ranks of an army of giants. In the pale moonlight I could have tilted at and run them through as things of life —ogres holding in captivity a maiden of the golden age.

Upon emerging from the cork wood saw two Spaniards concealed above a narrow ravine, and watching with alarmed interest what appeared to be a most desperate fight going on between a dozen or so dark, almost black, half-naked men, with long, unkempt hair. They were evidently not of the Spanish Gitano breed, but seemed to be of some Indian type. It certainly looked at first, from their tremendous excitement and the fierce way they rushed at and fell upon each other, as if there must be bloodshed—indeed, as if their tangled scalps would alone remain to mark the spot of a bloody fray. Upon closer observation, however, I could see that no knives were out. Truly this *pays de l'imprevu*, where a common greeting to the traveller is "*Vaya Vd. con Dios y que no haya novedad*," is the very land of knight errantry. Whether it was something in the air and scenery of this particular part, or the strange experiences of the day, I know not; but the gentle Don Quixote was continually in my mind. I am sure that if I had ridden in among them and demanded that they should cease brawling and acknowledge *instanter* the peerless beauty of my Dulcinea, the caitiffs would have yielded, and, after haranguing them upon the chivalry of Christ's religion, I might have sent them with ropes about their necks to await her sovereign pleasure.

Upon arriving at El Bosque, put up for the night at the *posada* "*San Antonio.*" Charming people, of the true mountain breed.

It is worth recording that in this place, mainly inhabited by peasantry corresponding to our agricultural labourers, there was, I observed, a *posada*-looking place, dignified by the name of the Summer Theatre, the pieces announced for representation happening to be "*Como un pez en aqua*" and "*Dios Consiente.*" I was not able to procure copies of these particular *cuentos*. There are many of them, however, represented in the *pueblos*, all in much the same style, and they afford immense delight to these simple-hearted folk. Here is a specimen :—

LA BUENA Y LA MALA FORTUNA.

Fernan.

Tio (Uncle) Romance, I want you to-day to tell me a tale.

Tio Romance.

What! another? Señor Don Fernan, I have already told your worship that my stories are not worth committing to paper. They are only fanciful ideas.

Fernan.

And I reply that doesn't matter; so cut along.

Tio Romance.

Señor ! They are only things of the street (*cosas de por la calle*).

Fernan.

Uncle Romance, every one to his taste. I tell you that you please me, and that much when you tell me a tale.

Tio Romance.

Say no more, señor. You have touched me in a soft place, and there is no refusing. My memory, however, now is so hazy that many things have almost gone from me, so I will recount to you something of recent date.[1]

Upon a rock which stands at the foot of a sierra there stands firmly placed a *pueblo*, like a nest of storks upon a tower.[2] I will not give the name—"Let the miracle be related without mentioning the name of the saint," as they say.

In this *pueblo* lived two men, who had been taken charge of respectively by Good and Bad Fortune. One had been named Don Joseph the Prosperous; the other, Uncle John Misery. Don Joseph commenced by selling in the streets linen and fine cloth; later on he set up a shop; then he took on a small farm. Indeed Fortune breathed upon him in such an unceasing manner that he very soon amassed one of the largest fortunes in the town. The señor was, moreover, in good repute, because he was not *barren* nor tight-fisted, but very charitable, and a good Chris-

---

[1] *Note by the Relater.*—And so recent, that even till quite lately the two characters introduced in this tale were living. The French say that in Paris wit flows along the streets. With greater reason can we say it pervades the fields of Andalucia.

[2] Storks' nests upon the out-buildings of *Cortijos*, and upon church towers are quite a feature of the country. They are never disturbed.

tian. **Money had** not puffed him up, nor his **great** wealth rendered him haughty. He was not arrogant, but plain, like the high road (*camino real*). He had no fancies, nor did he use high-flown expressions, as happens sometimes with those who assume fine speech. It **does not become** them, in spite **of** all their endeavours. **When you** least expect it, out comes some nonsense. In a word, Don Joseph and his household were good people, and in his house all were saints, down to the water-carrier.

They say, "*Donde no hay harina, todo es mohina*" ("Where there is **no** flour, all is animosity"); so all that the house of Uncle Misery contained was hunger, nakedness, wrangling, **screaming** children, and blows to hush them.

One day Don Joseph sent for Misery, who appeared **before** him in such **a state** that you couldn't touch him even with a pair of tongs, nor speak to **him** except at a distance, and it would have been quite worth while to have given him a *peseta* rather than see **him**. He had such a sour visage that one would rather have said "Good morning" from afar. He said **on** entering:

"Praised **be** God! **God protect your Honour**, Señor Don Joseph!"

"The same to you, man; but how **sour** and cross you look!"

"No wonder, Señor, when **I have two** yards of hunger, while my guts are trying to eat each other up. '*Barriga vacia todo es sequia*' ('All is dryness in an empty stomach'). Your Honour, **on the** other hand, is well filled out and satisfied—'*Barriga llena á Dios alaba*' ('A well-filled stomach praises God')."

"Yes, it is true. I have nothing to complain of."

"I should indeed think that your Honour was *requinto*,[1] for your stock always increases twentyfold; *le carga la marrana* (the sow is freighted).[2] Not that I am the *prosulta*[3] of misery."

"John, in this world there have always been and always will be those that laugh and those who weep. But let us come to the point. I have sent for you to ask you to go to the Palace of Fortune and tell my Fortune, on my behalf, that I am satisfied and don't want anything more. I will give you for going two hundred reals, that you may relieve your wants."

Instead of joyfully accepting this proposal and an opportunity the like of which had never come to him before, Cupidity entered into John Misery, and he said to Don Joseph:

"What, Señor! Two hundred reals are not sufficient to raise or lower any one. Remember that the Palace of Fortune is perched high up where Christ uttered the three cries and no one heard them. If I go along by the weir I shall get wet; if over the broken ground I shall encounter wolves and rugged paths.

---

[1] Uncle Misery means to say *contento*. Like Sancho Panza he is fond of using words of which he does not understand the meaning. *Requintar* is to superadd, and in music means to raise or lower the tone.

[2] This proverb means "You are in luck."

[3] This is his rendering of *Non plus ultra*.

Your Honour ought to give me three hundred reals, for the errand is well worth it."

Don Joseph had foreseen the slyness of John Misery. Nevertheless he told him he would give twelve dollars, and it was agreed to. Just as he was leaving, however, he turned and said to Don Joseph that twelve dollars was very little.

"Will you take nine?" quietly replied Don Joseph.

"Señor! Is your Honour jesting with me?" said John Misery. "I wouldn't go for twelve dollars, and now I am asked to go for nine!"

"Very well, don't go," said Don Joseph.

When Misery heard this reply he fairly staggered.

"What! am I to lose those nine dollars that I require so much?" said the poor fellow to himself. So, turning back, he told the prosperous one that he would go for the nine.

"Will you take six?" demanded Don Joseph.

"Well, indeed! this is rising from town crier to executioner,"[1] replied John Misery. "For six I will not go, anyhow."

"Very well, don't go," said Don Joseph.

John Misery went away; but he had scarcely reached the street when he thought better of it, for he sorely needed money. "The rich are those who

---

[1] That is to say, rising the wrong way. The executioner in Spain, not probably on account of his shedding blood, but from the Oriental idea of pollution, is held accursed, and loses all right to the title of Don.

kill or heal," he said, under his waistcoat, "and there is nothing for it but to lower one's ears. Would that I had gone for the twelve! Well says the proverb '*La codicia rompe el saco*' ('Cupidity breaks open the bag')." He once more returned and said to the prosperous one:

"Señor Don Joseph, necessity knows no law, I will go for the six *estiticos*."[1]

"Will you take three?" replied the rich man.

"Let the devil wear out a pair of shoes or crack his skull going up those craggy peaks for three wretched dollars for me! Farewell (*Con Dios*), Don Joseph!"

"Until I see you again, my son!"

Scarcely had John Misery gained the street when he pondered, "Am I to remain without those sixty reals—I who am not worth a farthing, and don't know where to get one?"

He hurried back and cried out from the door:

"Don Joseph! Look here, Señor! I will go for those three cursed dollars."

"Will you take one?" said the rich man.

"Yes, Señor!" replied John Misery, quicker than a pistol-shot, as he ran off ere Don Joseph had time to renew his proposal.

After climbing the rugged heights the whole day, he reached a rock so high and craggy that there was not foothold for a goat, and even the sunbeams slipped off.

On the summit of this rock was poised the Palace of Fortune, which was of alabaster, with doors of pure

---

[1] *Estiticos*—costive things, hence difficult to be obtained.

gold. When he gained the top he found himself in a courtyard like a royal *plaza*, full of flowers of every kind, evergreen grass and fruit-trees of all seasons. He at once began to call lustily for the Fortune of Don Joseph the Prosperous. A damsel came in answer to his summons, more brilliant than the sun, buxom, golden-haired and fair, each cheek like a rose each, eye like a star, and she carried more trinkets than a jeweller's shop.

"What do you want with me?" said this very fantastic maiden.

"Don Joseph the Prosperous has sent me to tell your Ladyship from him that he is satisfied and wants no more. Do you understand, beautiful alluring creature (*resalada sandunguera*)?"

"Well, tell him from me," replied the beauty, "that I will continue to load him with favours, whether he likes it or no, until he dies, because such is my sweet will. Do you hear? And now return the same way you came, or you will stink out my palace with misery."

"And has this bouquet of roses no little favour to confer on me, even if it be nothing more than a *cuarto* of spices?"

"I am not your Fortune, and can do nothing for you," replied the damsel; "but here at the back of my palace stands that of *your* Fortune. Go and have a colloquy with her."

Saying this she sped away, dancing like a whipping-top and singing like a canary.

Misery bounded out, turned round the corner, and came to the palace of his Fortune.

This dwelling was a heap of stones blacker than my hat. Between each crevice there was a viper and in each hole a snake.

"So this is where dwells my Fortune," said John Misery. "'As the bird is, so is the nest.' I shall call her, for I long to see her shining (*repulia*) face."

So he began to call out.

From among the ruins, in answer to his cries, came forth an old woman, uglier than she who deceived St. Anthony and stoned St. Stephen,[1] having a toothless mouth, and with bleared eyes bereft of eyelashes.

"What do you want with me?" demanded the old hag, in a voice like a wooden rattle.

"To send you to the devil, like the damned one you are," replied John Misery.

"Well, let me tell you," said the old woman, "that because you caught me napping you have earned a dollar. Had you not done so, not for the twenty would you have come."

All these *cuentos*, as related to this day, are full of proverbs more or less. There is also generally, as in the above specimen, some fun got out of the way

---

[1] SPANISH EDITOR'S NOTE.—This is an anachronism, for St. Stephen suffered martyrdom about the year A.D. 34, whilst St. Anthony died A.D. 361. Perhaps the personification of the evil woman is meant.

in which the unlettered are given to using fine words, the meaning of which they imperfectly understand, in a wrong or strained connection. The reader will observe the light which this throws upon the satire of Cervantes.

Upon leaving the *posada* in the morning, the daughter of the house, her mother standing by, with the grace and freedom of manner of the Spanish peasantry all their own—it was not French, it was not Italian, but distinctively Spanish—presented the parting traveller with a red rose. It accentuated the "*Vaya Vd. con Dios*" with which he was sent upon his way. That rose he has still within the leaves of his diary. It is dry, but whenever he looks at it now, in the English village where his lot is cast, it expands in the garden of memory once more in sunny Spain, and reminds him of a bright young human heart.

TRAVELLER'S JOY.

Ah! sweet blooming rose!
   With more *gracia* thou wast born
Than pen mortal can disclose.
But, ere summer sun hath left thee,
   Of light and warmth bereft thee,
     Thou must fade.
Ay de mi desventurado!
   That was born to suffer grief O!
From over the sea one sunny day
   I see thee Lolita, in tears!
But, ere I may *thy* griefs allay
   With a red, red rose,
     I see me sadly die.

The way to the next *pueblo*, Buonomohema, lies through the most sublime scenery, the travelling, however, being decidedly dangerous. Above one rises the lofty sierra, not bald, but covered enough to please the eye with every conceivable shade of green, height above height, the very summit now, in the early morning, being partly hidden in the Cirrus-like clouds formed by the fast-vanishing morning dew—a solitary eagle king of the vast solitude. Beneath one, mighty depth descends beyond depth, at times the path, rounding some boulder, being so narrow that one shudders. Close to the eye little saxafrages and sedums of many sorts and kinds wander in loving tenacity over the rocks. It all expressed to my wondering senses the very *abandon* of the Almighty glorying in His works both great and small. I cannot imagine anything more imposing in the way of scenery. If hereafter I shall ever see the city whose gates are of pearl, beryl, topaz, chrysoprasus, and amethyst, I only hope they may be nearly all clothed with green.

Upon nearing Buonomohema, came

up with an old woman, evidently one of the poorest of the poor, and hard-featured, leading a donkey loaded with vegetables. Always on the look-out for stores for the commissariat, I asked her if she could let me have some. Wretch that I was, I selected the best of her stock, of course intending to pay her handsomely. She would take nothing, however, declining with so much dignity and gentleness that I could no more hope to force payment upon her than upon the first lady in the land. Arrived about 8.30. Brought out my tea, together with those ill-gotten lettuces and onions; the host of the *posada* provided hot water; a sweet, black-eyed child of about fourteen, with a red rose in her hair, waited upon us, and we had a jolly breakfast—far happier than kings.

THE BLACK-EYED CHILD.

Maiden, who hast of Aprils seen,
  With not a winter in between,
    But scarce fourteen :
Beautiful as morning star,
    As the Graces *Graciosa*,
    As angel pure *hermosa*,
That with outstretched wings o'er thy smiling sleep
Descends, when night descends, his faithful watch to keep !
    Listen, little maiden, listen ; nay,
      From my counsel do not fly
        To chase yon painted butterfly.
  For, if on my words you'll some time ponder,
      Never shall the fates portend,
      But light and joy unto the end.
Thy hopes now in heaven centre, thy love to thy sweet mother holds,
Thy yearnings butterflies, thy world thine own village enfolds.
    But soon another love, I trow,
    Thou'lt feel a vague desire to know
      Whether mother will have it or no.
    While other hopes will in thy bosom nestle,
      To other worlds, and other yearning
        Thy thoughts be turning.
'Tis well, dear child. When this tender glow comes to thee
Consecrate it all to God who made thee ;

> Let thy pure bosom be its home;
> Let it not free, unfettered roam—
> Till thy *novio* sings to thee!
> Put not thy trust in men, now mark me well,
> Though we should strum and pine, and swear, and say
> A thousand, thousand times, Hey day!
> I love thee for ever and a day.

After breakfast looked in at the village smithy, where I observed that the well-made shoes are put on cold, without any paring of the hoof. The frank young smith was much interested in pointing out through the field-glasses the winding track for Grazalema through the mountains.

> "El que presume de honra
> Es porque carece de ella,
> Aquel que no tiene capa
> Se acuerda de Grazalema,"
>
> ("He who vaunts his honour
> 'Tis because he lacks it;
> He who has no Capa
> Let him remember Grazalema,")

says the *copla*, Grazalema being famous for its *capas*, the universal Spanish cloak. Soon after leaving Buonomohema it came on to rain in torrents—and it can rain, too, in the Sierras! The water, rushing down the clefts of the mountains at one point, completely washed away all traces of the track. The little compass attached to the watch-chain I now found of the greatest use, as I had done on former rides. Indeed I should prefer not to go far into the Sierras without one. The weather cleared as suddenly as it had become overcast, and Grazalema came into view gleaming in the bright sunshine. Unlike most of the mountain *pueblos*, it is situated in a valley. One looks down upon Grazalema from the heights. On the outskirts were women, dotted about here and there up the mountain side, washing clothes (without soap) in the sparkling crystal stream. The bright *pañuelas*, like flowers among the now glistening foliage, were in harmony with the bright voices of the women as they sang at their work :—

>Tengo un amante hechichero,
>Que vale mas que un Peru,
>Y su officio es de Torero
>Torerito y Andaluz.
>
>(I have a charming lover
>Worth more than a Peru,
>And he is a bull fighter,
>A little bull fighter and Andaluz.)
>
>Si tu marido es celoso,
>Dála a comer chicharrones
>Y veras con la manteca
>Que suavito te se pone.
>
>(If your husband is cranky
>Give him *chicharrones* for dinner
>And see, as the sweet fat goes down,
>How sweet he will become to you.)

Para los hombres chicos
Viene la leva ;
Yo me meteré al mio
En el faltriquera.

(The pressgang is out
Looking for little men ;
I shall put mine
In my pocket.)

In the eventide they would, maybe, return to their mates together, singing a song in the following strain :—

LA MAMITA.[1]

La vecina de enfrente
Mamita mia
Mira mi casa

---

[1] Simple and almost nonsensical as these words may appear when put down upon cold paper (a distinction with which they have probably never before been honoured), there is a wonderful charm about the song when sung to the guitar by one to the manner born. My friend, Miss Mariana Monteiro, the accomplished authoress of " Legends of the Basque Provinces " (Fisher Unwin), has kindly written down for me such of the words as she remembered. The music expresses, in a delightful manner, the gay, careless, jaunty walk home after the day's work in the open air.

Y no mira la suza
  Mamita mia
Que se le abraza.

Vamonos à acostar
Vamonos à dormir
Tu llevaras la Manta
  Mamita mia
Y yo el candil.

Y el candil sin aceite
  Mamita mia
Coma ha de lucir !

De una leve chispa,
  Mamita mia
No hize caso
Se originó la llama
  Mamita mia
En que me abrazo.

Mi marido me dice
  Mamita mia
Que jo me componga !
  Que queria ese demonio
  Mamita mia !
Que yo me ponga !

Translation :—

THE LITTLE MOTHER.

Neighbour over the way,
  Little mother,

Stares at my house,
And doesn't see,
    Little Mother,
That her own is in flames!

Let us go to bed,
    Little mother!
Let us go to sleep—
You shall take the blanket,
    Little mother,
And I'll take the lamp.[1]

But the lamp,
    Little mother,
Has no oil;
  And if without oil,
    Little mother,
How can it burn?

A little tiny spark,
    Little mother,
I heeded not.
  From it arose,
    Little mother,
The flames in which I burn.

My husband bids me,
    Little mother
To dress gaily.

---

[1] *Candil* is an egg-shaped lamp, or rather lantern, the top division being movable. It has a wick, and is fed with olive oil.

> What may it please that devil,
>   Little mother,
> That I should put on?

From Grazalema the way to Ronda again lies through the wildest scenery. Another deluge of rain washed away all traces of the track. Got on with a muleteer, however, and pushed on, wet to the skin of course, but ready to sing as usual. Five minutes after the storm had ceased, in a very wild and lonely spot, came suddenly upon two *Guardias*, who had already lit a blazing fire (how I cannot think), and were carefully examining their arms and ammunition, drying and cleaning their clothes, and getting themselves again into that neat and trim order for which they are famous.

It is impossible to pass by the *Guardia*

Civiles in any notice of the Sierras as they are to-day. Somewhere about the time our own "Bobbies" were instituted, this corps was organised by the Spanish poet, Martinez de la Rosa, Prime Minister to Queen Christina. He had himself been robbed by brigands in the Sierras, and, as a result, when he acquired power, evolved this scheme for ridding his country of the pest of brigandage. And the back of brigandage, as an institution, they have undoubtedly broken. This is agreeably brought to mind by the mortuary crosses one comes across at times in the wildest parts of the Sierras. For my part, mindful of the line from Horace, "*Cantabit vacuus coram ladrone viator,*" I had taken little money in my belt; but still, one cannot well stick an advertisement of one's impecuniosity up in one's hat. Our own bobbies have truncheons; these men have sword, rifle, revolver, and power to use them, too, at their own discretion. As this power is never abused, it is evident that these men must have set before them a very high moral standard. When one glances at the very remarkable Rules and Regulations of the force, one sees at once that they are an outcome of poetic instinct. No cynic could, with a serious face, in this nineteenth century, have ever taken in hand the formation of a corps upon a basis which, *mutatis mutandis*, might have served for the Hospitallers of St. John. But that the corps has proved a great practical success in the land of Cervantes no one for a moment doubts. And it is no slight compliment to Spain to say that probably such a force, on such a basis, and with such powers, could not exist in any other country of Europe. I have come across an anonymous popular *cantar* which sings the praises of the Civil Guards. It is too long to give here. The following are the concluding lines. They are given as evidence of the popular esteem into which the force has worked its way, by a strict adherence to its fundamental rules.

LA GUARDIA CIVIL.

¡ Feliz el pueblo que puede
dormir en la confianza
de que hay un ángel custodio
que le cubre con sus alas !
Ya reduzcan á cenizas
los edificios las llamas,
ya la corriente del rio
las poblaciones invada,
ya el infeliz trajinero
se hunda en simas ó barrancas,

> ya carezca el caminante
> de alimento ó de posada,
> ya el puñal del asesino
> atente á la vida humana,
> siempre la Guardia Civil
> cual la paloma del arca
> en medio del cataclismo
> es nuncio de la esperanza,
> y por eso en todas partes
> bendiciones la acompañan,
> por eso Dios la protege
> cuando al peligro se lanza,
> por eso la canto yo
> con el corazon y el alma
> Viva la Guardia Civile
> Porque es la Gloria de España.

I also observed during Holy Week in Xerez that the post of honour as supporters of the *Andas*, on which were carried the *Pasos* of the Virgin, was conceded to the Civil Guard.

Of course a force which beareth not the sword in vain, and is a terror to evil-doers, has not wanted detractors. They have been called *Polizones* (French *polissons*), and it has been said that they are employed by a corrupt government for purposes of oppression and to stifle the expression of public opinion. I do not believe it. Neither do I think that any one seriously does so. Only the other day I read an account in the *Illustrated London News* of an *emeute* at a *Fiesta de Toros* at Linares, in the Province of Jaen. The Civil Guards refused, at the Mayor's behest, to quell the disturbance with the bayonet. This may be explained by a reference to Rules 30 and 31 below.

Observe how the French and Russian system of *espionage* is repudiated.

GENERAL DUTIES OF THE CIVIL GUARDS.

1. Honour must afford the chief motive for the Civil Guard, to be preserved intact and without a flaw. Once gone, honour can never be regained.

2. The first condition of existence of a force like that of the Civil Guards is that its *prestige* and *morale* should be of the highest. Without these such a force cannot exist. [I should think not!]

3. The force must be an example to the country of neatness, order, bearing, good morals, and spotless honour.

5. Always faithful to duty, calm and composed in danger, while performing its duties with firmness, dignity, gentleness, and prudence, the Civil Guard will be more respected than any force that resorts to threats and violence.

6. Each individual member of the force, whether private or officer, must be prudent and patient, without weakness, firm without severity, courteous without servility, and a man *to be feared only by evil-doers and haters of order.*

8. The Civil Guard ought to be regarded as the protector of the afflicted, inspiring confidence when seen approaching. The man attacked by assassins must hail his coming as his best deliverer. The man whose house is on fire must see before him escape from peril and the flames put out when the Civil Guard arrives upon the scene. The man swept away by the winter torrent must feel himself close to the shore when he sees the glazed helmet and blue tunic of the Civil Guard approaching. For the Civil Guard must freely give his life for the good of any sufferer.

9. Whenever a member of the Civil Guard has the great good fortune to render a service to any one he must never accept a reward, if offered, bearing in mind that he has done nothing but his simple duty.

But, apart from money, should he be offered a keepsake, let him not regard such keepsake as in any sense a reward, but as nothing more than a token of gratitude, the approval of his own conscience being his only reward. In this way the Civil Guard will retain in his breast the pride of honour, for his great aim will be to satisfy his own conscience and win the esteem and confidence of all.

11. Whether stationed in the capital of his country or in the loneliest *despoblado*, the Civil Guard must never go out without having his hair neatly cut, his beard being shaved at least once every other day, his face and hands washed scrupulously clean, his nails trimmed and cleaned, the leather of his boots, accoutrements, and arms lustrous and brilliant, and his coat brushed and neatly mended if it should have been torn.

16. The Civil Guard will be attentive to all, always yielding the right side of the street, not only to his own officers, but to the authorities of the town whether civil or military. But especially he will be polite to all ladies. By acting thus his bearing will be a pattern of subordination and deference to some; to others of studied politeness; and for all an example of good breeding.

19. The Civil Guard will never enter any house or dwelling of any sort or kind without saying "By your leave," or "Give me leave," and he will never call any one *patron* or *patrona*, as do common soldiers. He will enter a house hat in hand, and keep it in his hand until he takes his departure.

24. Should the Civil Guard discover a man in the

road so severely wounded that he may die before the next village is reached he must then and there take his declaration.

27. The Civil Guard will refrain with the greatest scrupulousness from drawing near to listen to the conversation of any knot of people in street, shop, casino, or private house, for this would be an act of *espionage*, altogether outside the office and beneath the dignity of any member of the force.

30. The Civil Guard is not a dependent of the Justice of the place where he is stationed; but he must give his services, if required by the civil authority, and that *according to his own rules.*

31. The Civil Guard, in certain cases, if he should see the civil authorities of any town allowing evils to exist which they might check, must report to the highest authority, the Governor of the Province.

The approach to Ronda by the mule track is somewhat dangerous travelling, the descent to the *carretera,* about a mile from the city, being especially rocky and bad. The aspect of this mountain stronghold is again very striking. It is built upon the tops of two mountains *en echelon.* A very deep ravine divides them, and across this ravine there is a very solidly-built viaduct connecting the two portions of the city. Put up at a *posada* close to this viaduct.

I can understand the term *Borrico* now. Not "*Arré Burra*," but "*Arré Borrico*" ("Get on, *little* ass") is the universal cry of the drivers of the long strings of donkeys with their wonderfully well-balanced burdens. Why always "*little* ass"? I had often asked myself. On looking round this *posada*, crowded at the time with visitors to the fair, I saw many mules, a very few horses (*equus major*), and very many donkeys (*equus minor*). The latter, with their long, soft ears, and sweet, intelligent faces ranged round the stalls, taking in all that goes on, are so useful, so hardy and willing, and so adapted to the requirements of the country that the endearing term "little ass" really suggests itself to one. Perhaps it would be better if he would hold his tongue. But even this struck me (I don't know whether it would strike anybody else) as being singularly in harmony with the surroundings. After gazing at all that goes on with his brown, open, wise-looking eyes for a long time, something ludicrous seems to strike him, and he laughs a hearty laugh. It is contagious. Here and there others join in " Ah! ah! ah! Did your Grace see that Manuel of ours and Don Ricardo? Capital joke, wasn't it?" And then all are quiet and demure again for a little time. Anon the humours of the ever-shifting scene tickle him again, and he laughs once more. The horses and mules have more sense, are more decorous and sober, but are not so human,

Upon asking *el Señor Dueño* if he had a very good bedroom, "*Hombré*" said he, shrugging his shoulders with good-humoured frankness, "*es bueno.*" It was at least nicely whitewashed, the bed-linen as white as snow, and there were no individuals of the genus *pulex*. Acting under advice, and after reading accounts of Spanish travel, I had put some flea-powder among my *impedimenta*, but did not have to use it once during my experience of Andalucian *posadas*. That was my experience, and I have thought it well to record it. I cannot answer for the experiences of others. Eventually secured a good dinner of chicken (without garlic), *carne*, kidneys, salad, and Val de Penas wine —the same blood-red wine that Don Quixote stabbed in the pig-skin. Having satisfied the cravings of appetite, descended through the cheerful, humming crowd, to the courtyard below. Muleteers (each with his relic lying upon his brown breast, I'll be bound)— *arrieros*—and whole families, who had come in from the *pueblos*, were lying about on the bare, unpaved ground anywhere, wrapped up snugly in blankets and rugs, and sleeping soundly through all the noise and bustle—a sleep which one with the fateful riches of Peru upon his shoulders might envy. I surveyed them carefully for some time, but did not see one whose sleep was in the slightest degree disturbed.

Presently, as the shades of night began to fall, about twenty little claret-coloured pigs—not dirty things, but clean as cats—came trotting in of their own accord from the mountains, jumping playfully over the sleepers with the utmost confidence, and making their way to the yard beyond. Their actions said, as plainly as actions could speak, "There's no place like home, sweet home"—after grubbing all day up on the mountains. For I cannot imagine a pig for ever imprisoned in a dirty sty a few feet square giving vent to such sentiments; rather do I imagine his saying, "Anywhere, anywhere out of my sty." Nay, I can fancy his actually longing to be made into savoury pork—anything rather than his forced unsavoury surroundings. These pigs I had seen on the mountains in thousands. I was told that as the time for bed draws near, each lot trot off to their own home with unerring certainty, and bring their tails behind them. They are very seldom lost.

Wherein lies the charm of a Spanish *posada?* That there is a charm most intelligent travellers will acknowledge. Wherein does it consist? Common luxuries are absurdly wanting. I think it must lie in the healing sense that comes over one of the brotherhood of man. Jews, Turks, infidels, and heretics may here lie down in peace with the orthodox Catholic. The *Odium Theologicum* which, whatever one may say, seems to be innate in the human breast, does not enter here. It is quite shut out. One feels it, and knows it. And then, strangely in harmony with this line of thought, is not one continually reminded of the manger, converted, perforce, into a cradle, "because they

112   THE HEART AND SONGS OF

had no room for them in the inn"? Does not the charm consist in this? If so, then one can easily account for being so readily able to do, for a little time, without those hundred and one adjuncts of civilisation which we insensibly come to look upon as among the very necessaries of life.

DE NOCHE BUENA.

La Vir-gen qui-so sen-tar-se á la som-bra de un oli-var, y se vol-vie-ron las ho-jas á ver re-cien na-ci-do que tó-ma-las allá, tó-ma-las ba-bas ver-des que si y que ya mo-li-ne-ro que el a-gua no te ha de fal-tar. Ji, ja, ja, ja, ja, ja, ja.

(The Virgin sat herself
Beneath the shade of an olive,
And the leaves bent down
To gaze on the new-born babe.
Take the olives, take the beans,
Green as they are, tell the
Miller the
Water will not fail him ever more.
  La ! la ! la !)

 En el portal de Belen
Gitanitos han entrado,
Y al niño recien nacido
Los pañales le han quitado
  ¡ Picaros Gitanos,
  Caras de Aceitunas
  No han dejado al niño
  Ropita ninguna !

(Into the porch of Bethlehem
Little gipsies have entered
And stolen the swaddling clothes
Of the new-born babe.
  Knavish *Gitanos*,
  With olive faces !
  They have not left the child
  A single garment.)

 A grandes ciudades
V^{ed} como no va,
prefiriendo á ellas
un pobre portal.

·(To great cities
Your grace (*usted*) does not go,
Preferring to them
A poor porch.)

La Virgen Maria
Va pesando nieve,
pudiendo pisar
rosas y claveles.

(The Virgin Mary
Goes treading on the snow,
When she should be treading
On roses and carnations.)

La Virgen se fué á lavar
Lús manas blancas al rio ;
El sol se quedó parado
La mar perdió su ruido.

(The Virgin washed
Her white hands in the river ;
The sun began to appear,
The sea became calm.)

Los pastores de Belen
Todo juntos van por leña,
Para calentar al niño,
Que nació la noche buena.

(The shepherds of Bethlehem
Go together to look for fuel,
To warm the child
That was born on the Good night.)

En el portal de Belen
Ha nacido un manolito,
Que dicen que es mas bonito
Que Juanito el de Isabel.

(In the porch of Bethlehem
There is born a man child,
Who they say is more pretty
Than Isabel's little Juan.)

Todos le llevan al niño,
Yo no tengo que llevarle,
Le llevaré el corazon
Que le sirva de pañales.

(All bring gifts for the babe,
I have nothing to bring;
I'll give Him my heart
To wrap Him in.)

En el portal de Belen
Hay estrella, sol, y luna,
La Virgen y San José,
Y el niño que está en la cuna.

(In the porch of Bethlehem
There is a star, sun, and moon
The Virgin and St. Joseph
And the child in the cradle.)

Una pandereta suena,
Yo no sé por dónde va,
Camina para Belen
Hasta llegar al portal.

Al ruido que llevaba,
El Santo José salió ;
No me desperteis al niño,
Que ahora poco se durmió.
　Lo ha dormido entre sus brazos
Aquella que lo parió,
Y su canto era tan dulce,
Que pudo dormir á Dios.

(A timbrel is heard,
I know not whither bound,
It travels on to Bethlehem
Until it reaches the shed.
　At the noise it made
Saint Joseph rushed out.
Do not awaken the Babe
For He has just gone to sleep.
　He is asleep in the arms
Of her who bore Him.
Her lullaby was so sweet
That it made God slumber.)

En Belen tocan á fuego,
Del portal sale la llama ;
Y es que alli ha nacido aquel
¡ Que en llamas de amor sé abrasa.

(In Bethlehem the fire-bell rings,
From the porch flames are issuing ;
It is that there is born He
Who in flames of love is consumed.)

Esta noche nace el niño
Entre la papa y el hielo.
¡ Quien pudiera, niño mio,
Vestirte de terciopelo !

(This night was born the child
Between the straw and the frost.
Thou mightest, my child,
Have been clothed in velvet !)

En un portalito oscuro,
Llenito de telerañas
Entre la mula y el buey
Nació el Redentor de almas.
    La mula le gruñe
  El buey le bajea
  Y el niño de Dios
  Dormido se queda.

(In an obscure shed,
Littered with trifles,
Between the mule and the ox,
Was born the Saviour of souls.
    The mule creaked,
  The ox lowed,
  And the Child of God
  Continued to sleep.)

To Bethlehem, shepherds, to Bethlehem,
To see the grand child of Anna,
Who leads a lion bound
With a cord of wool.
    Taralala, taralali,
    Taralali, taralala.

After breakfast strolled out to the famous Ronda fair. Everywhere there was an airy briskness as of the mountain top. All were unconsciously acting upon the advice of Horace:—

"*Dona presentis cape lætus horæ;*"

or of Scripture if you will :—

"Sufficient unto the day is the evil thereof."

Lines of booths were arranged in long rows, where all sorts of toys, *confiteria*, castanets, bells, antique brasswork, and, still most characteristic of all, Andalucian horse, mule, and donkey trappings, leggings, gaiters, &c., were sold. Further on men in front of booths were encouraging people to "walk up," much in the same way as at home. There was also the quack doctor and cheap Jack, with all sorts of devices for trying one's luck. There, too, was the ballad singer, singing a "*Relacion Andaluz*," printed in exactly the same style and headed by exactly the same sort of rough woodcuts as the stories of "Jack the Giant Killer," and so on, in old

English chap-books. I bought one of these ballads from the man, but am quite unable to translate it on account of the phonetic spelling. Cadiz is written *Cai;* Seville, *Ceviya;* Gibraltar, *Gibrarta.* It seemed to amuse the listeners immensely. The lines "*Montañas,*" at the beginning of this book were taken from a precisely similar chap-book. I assume, therefore, that the phonetic spelling is not always adopted.

What is that hanging over the door of yonder house? A bunch of vine twigs. It was an invitation to enter. It was as if the proprietor, having finished his harvest, had just wiped his brow, tied together with the tendrils a few of the broken vine stems, and had hung them up outside his door as an announcement to wearied sinners, " The

UPS AND DOWNS.

wine crop has been gathered in, the grapes have been crushed, the must has been collected, there is still old wine in the *amphoræ*, enter and drink that which maketh glad the heart of man." [1]

Upon entering to take a glass in the quiet shade, under a growing vine, I found that they had some really excellent *Vino de Xerez* (sherry). This is a very dear wine, as things go in Spain,

---

[1] This simple invitatory sign was, I believe, common in happier times in what was then merry England.

"Some ale-houses upon the road I saw,
And some with bushes, showing they wine did draw."
   Poor Robin's Perambulations, 1678.

Now the hot pedestrian is impudently entrapped into the publican's den by silly tinsel announcements, "Try our noted Old Tom"; "Mountain Dew" whiskey; "Orange" gin. I shouldn't be surprised to see "Mothers' Milk" brandy soon. He is then made to stand up square before a pewter counter, and—*ut capitis minor*—told to shut his eyes and "swallow" whatever is put before him.

and is not much sought after by Spaniards. The *dueño* explained that he was enabled to keep it and sell it cheap because, as he kept his own *Madre Vino*, he simply bought the *musto* and "educated" it himself. Although I took a glass of sherry on this occasion, I much prefer the "innocent," cheap, and thirst-quenching *manzanilla*.[1]

I thought, but only for one brief moment, of Horace quaffing the Massic in the cool shade—I say for one brief moment only, for Horace was not a native of these Sierras. "Bacchus, ever young and fair," has never here been worshipped as a deity. He has been

---

[1] This wine is made from unripe grapes, grown on a poor soil. It is said to be very wholesome and to possess tonic properties of a high order, as I certainly found to be the case. The taste is very slightly bitter, resembling that of camomile flowers (Sp. *Manzanilla*), whence the name.

relegated to his proper place as a happy, cheerful, bright attendant upon his pure and sparkling mistress *aqua fresca*. There is an entire absence in this land of wine of those drinking songs common to more northern nations. In the mountain solitudes those improvised *coplas* of the goatherd and the muleteer touch on anything but wine.

The horse fair is held just outside the town, three long rows of booths covered with canvas and boughs being erected for the purpose. The horses did not seem to me to be first-rate. I might have picked up many a Rozinante. Probably the best had been sold on the first days of the fair. A *chulan*, as the Gitano horse dealer is called, came to me with a 20 *peseta* note, and asked if it was genuine. I thought at first he was going to try on the confidence trick. It appeared, however, that he had just had the note tendered to him by a purchaser of whose honesty he did not feel quite sure. It is curious how everywhere rascality seems to centre round the horse, the most generous of animals. I should like to hear *Babieca* and *Rozinante* discuss the matter.[1]

Although when in Spain, out of respect for a faith which was not mine, I, as a rule, refrained from gazing, in idle curiosity, around the churches; I did

---

[1] *Babieca* was the Cid's famous horse :—

> "Troth it goodly was and pleasant
> To behold him at their head,
> All in mail on Babieca,
> And to list the words he said."

Rozinante was the no less famous horse of another Spanish hero. In some Spanish lines which I have seen somewhere, but cannot remember, the two are represented as meeting and conversing about their masters.

leave the fun of the fair to enter one here for a few moments' rest. Strung before different images of saints were great numbers of *ex-votos* (many more than I had ever seen anywhere else)—arms, legs, eyes, pigs, donkeys, mules, all cut out of tin. Also a long lock of hair tied with blue ribbons—a tell-tale offering.

> " He promised to buy me a bunch of blue ribbons
> To tie up my bonny brown hair."

And he didn't come back. Poor Maraquita!

Thence to the Plaza de Toros, which, unlike any I had yet seen, was of stone. It is said to be one of the most ancient in Spain, although this, I believe, is disputed. At all events it looks ancient, and recalls to the mind the time when knights and gentlemen entered the arena upon the best of horses, trained to swerve from the rush of the bull and not forced to meet it blindfold, as at present. It was built at the expense of the *Rael Maestranza*, the oldest of the noble orders of Spain.

Outside the arena saw some boys playing at *Toro*. They are always at it. The village youngster in the illustration, standing in the attitude of an *espada* in the final scene of the *Fiesta* before a *buey de carreta* (*faute de mieux*) —one of the mildest and meekest of quadrupeds — has found his vocation. Everything is done in order. Observe the youngster to the right acting as *chulo*, and prepared for any emergency, while the spectators on the cart—the *aficionadas*—are watching with a critical eye and discussing in correct Tauromachian

CHILDREN PLAYING.

style the attitude of the *espada*, the breeding and character of *Toro*, doubtless drawing upon their imagination for the latter.

In the illustration on p. 121 it will be observed that our hero is on the horns of a dilemma. He has found this animal rather different to the *buey de carreta*. Well, there are ups and downs in all pursuits. Sometimes these *embolados*—bulls whose horns have been blunted—are let into the Plaza for the amusement of any boys and youths who may choose to enter. They go frantic with excitement, and try their hand at all the phases of the real thing. Our hero apparently has been practising *el capeo*, or the challenge, so called because *capas* are used to allure the bull and make him come on. In the real bullfight *Toro* is practically doomed from the first. However brave a fight he may make of it, the gaily-decked mules are harnessed and in waiting, certain to be required, in a few moments, to drag out the body of the slain warrior. Here, however, he has it all his own way. If there were only an audience of some few thousand bulls, I can imagine the waving of tails and tremendous excitement at this moment, as the would-be *torero* is "hoist with his own *pétard*."

These *novilladas* take place in every Plaza de Toros, but are discountenanced by real Tauromachians as leading to broken bones and bloodshed, which they certainly do. But oh! the bulls, how they must enjoy the fun!

Our little friend has descended, let us hope, from his airy situation with only a few broken bones. His next rise in the world will perhaps be admittance into the Tauromachian School at Seville. In the illustration (page 183) the famous *Maestro* Pedro Romero is represented instructing the boy how to place the final sword-thrust in accordance with the strict canons of the art.

In the next illustration (page 193) he has attained the object of his ambition. Before the eyes of thousands of spectators he has accomplished the most difficult feat of all *una estocada a un tiempo*—the death-thrust at the first onset. Henceforth he will be placed in the first rank as an *espada*, be the idol of the multitude during his manhood's prime, and in old age fight his battles o'er again before a new generation in his native village.

In the evening entered a sort of *café* of which there were many. At one end a small platform was raised, on which a woman was dancing. When she had finished a peasant from the audience mounted the platform, and after a short period of silence—a sad look upon his bronzed face—clapped his hands in measured time for a while, and then broke out into a wild, plaintive song, the words and meaning of which, however, I could not catch. When he had finished, two other men, also from the audience, just as they were, danced with castanets. One of them was certainly between sixty and seventy. The dancing of the woman (a hired woman probably) I had seen on entering was more daringly voluptuous than that of the honest peasant-girls I had seen dance in the open air. But the dancing of the men! Its freedom, spontaneity, and grace were things to envy. Why, with sorrow I confess that I could no more do such a thing than I could fly. Could you, either in act or spirit, gentle reader? And you of threescore years, could you? Alas! I suspect the heart is scrunched out of us by our railways, &c., &c. They bring us many luxuries, but at what a price! There they are in that weary London of ours—on the earth, under the earth, coiled all round her vitals, blear-eyed monsters with sulphurous breath. Looking over an old number of the *Illustrated London News* the other day, I noticed an illustration of the opening of one of the earliest of our railways. There were banners displayed, " Railways and Civilisation," and there was a cocksure air about the whole proceedings. Well, after seeing these *Rondenos* dance and sing in their mountain home, I doubt whether "railways and civilisation" have added to the joy of life after all. Bravo China! You have the sense to know it![1]

In the early morning departed for Benoacaz (pronounced Benoahé). About a league from Ronda came to a booth of twigs near a little cottage or hut—just the place for a sylvan breakfast. The ever-courteous peasants came out and supplied a saucepan (the nearest approach to a teapot) and hot water for the tea; the *alforjas* yielded up bread and ham, and the claims of appetite

[1] Since penning the above lines, I have heard that the snort and screech of the infernal steam-engine are now heard in Virgin Ronda—fit prelude to indigestion, introspection, and all the blues of civilisation. *Caetera mitte loqui.*

were satisfied. While breakfasting two *guardias*, fine handsome fellows, entered and took their morning glass of *aquardiente*, and afterwards accepted a cup of tea—the drink of the *Inglez*. An *Andaluz*, on horseback, rode up in a great state of mind, and spoke to our peasant. Two mules had been stolen, and he was making search for them in all directions. A troupe of typical Spanish gipsies afterwards went by, one of the women especially, a handsome jade, casting glances at us with her fine, large, black, heathen eyes. Our host, observing them, said *sotto voce*, " The mules are seven leagues from here—*yo lo creo*—they are people of bad blood," meaning to say that the gipsies knew where the mules were.

What power there is in the human

eye! A belief in the evil eye is common here, derived perhaps from the Moors, among whom it is universal. May there not be a foundation for this belief in the subtle power of human influence (taking the literal meaning of the word) which escapes through the open windows, the eyes? It has, moreover, often struck me as strange how a person, with his back turned to one, perhaps, at whom one may be looking, will turn round, apparently conscious that you have been looking at him. It is also a common expression to say, "I *felt* he was looking at me." This power of the eye, I suppose, like that of the tongue, may be exercised for good as well as evil.

But, although our host thus anathematised the gipsies, to affect many of their ways and modes of thought and expression has long been considered "the thing" in Andalucia, especially in the province of Seville. It is not surprising, therefore, to find traces of the influence of the *Cantes Flamencos*, as the songs of the gipsies are called, upon much of Spanish song. On the other hand, contact with the objective worship of the Spanish Church has furnished images and colour to the *gitano*, but nothing more. He has grasped nothing more that it might have taught him. And so it comes to pass that complaints of the exceeding bitterness of death, and the separation of *compadres* which it causes, remains the dominant note. It is unrelieved by any ray or trace of Christian hope. I well remember having this brought to mind once in the neighbourhood of Trebujena, on observing a group of *gitanos* on their way to the burying of a dead *compadre*. There was a weird intensity about their grief, which might have brought home to the most thoughtless the meaning of his baptism into the bosom of the great Christian family. But while, as I have said, this would appear to be the dominant note, it is not the only note. Some of their songs are joyous, while some lend themselves to the dance. But the most characteristic are fiercely tragic.

The following *Sequidillas Jitanas* would be sung in the following style. First, the singer, with a dreamy, far-away look on his face, claps his hands together with a slow movement for a considerable time before opening his mouth. There is then a long drawn out "Ay." After which the voice pauses. More slow clapping of hands follows, and then the Sequidilla begins.

    Little Mother of Consolation
      May thy kindness Divine
        Never leave me
      In this grief to repine.

    A curse upon thee, Death
      For thy dread dominion,
    My comrade thou hast plucked from my side,
      And my little, little son.

    If thou lov'st me
      As I love thee,
    It appears to me, girl,
      This earth a heaven would be.

    As I was telling my beads,
      While the dawn was red,
    I saw approach the Mother of my soul
      With arms outspread.

    Dare you take on another lover?
      Commend him to God for ever;
    For with a single blow
      His heart in twain I'll sever.

    The little griefs I suffered,
      She has driven all away,
    With the graces of her person
      And the sweetness of her way.

Upon departing, our host would accept nothing in payment. I offered the money to a sweet little dark-eyed child, his daughter. She also was instinctively too proud to take it. She had a naked doll in her hand. When I begged that they would at least allow me to present the doll with a *camisa*, or shirt, they laughed heartily, but would take nothing more than a *pero grande* for the purpose of purchasing one.

Soon afterwards, near a swollen stream, came upon a murdered man's cross, of stone. The inscription upon it, as far as I could decipher it, was as follows:—

<pre>
"M I M
 O A N
 T O N I
O R O D I I
   1848."
</pre>

An old peasant told me he remembered the man. He was shot in the mouth.

The scenery now was of the wildest and grandest, the little sedums and saxafrages, moreover, near to the eye, seeming to abound here more than ever. I recognised great rambling masses of *Saxafraga sponhenica, Sedum reflexum, Sedum rupestre*. Perhaps it is the abundance of these that helps to give the pleasing bloom and varying tone to the near distance. The tinkle, tinkle, of the mule bells; the song of a muleteer, singing like an angel (although I don't suppose he was quite that), seated sideways upon the leading mule; the red fringes of his *alforjas* and trappings appearing and disappearing in the winding track above; all these sights and sounds were strikingly in harmony with the surroundings. And that man's voice, plaintive and sad, like the free winds of heaven, awakes the echoes. Why does he sing? Well, for one thing, he sings to keep his mules in heart; and they do follow him, evidently in sympathy. Poor things! their own attempts at singing are such miserable failures, being neither the braying nor the neighing of either of their progenitors, but a sort of squeak—between the two. And so they very properly let Manuel do the singing, while they contentedly listen the livelong day, and forget the fatigues of their long journeys—lost in wonder at the glorious human voice giving expression to articulate human language.[1]

[1] Probably few people realise the power, not only of the human voice, but of articulate human

And for another reason; there is a saying, "*Quien cantar, su mal espanta*" ("He who sings, his grief allays"). He sings because he is alone under the blue sky of his beloved Andalucia, and sing he must. Here is a *copla* taken down from the lips of a muleteer. It is amusingly frank.

language upon the brute creation. I once had a colley from the Scotch highlands to whom I was accustomed to talk, not in doggy language, but as one would talk to a human being. The interested expression in his brown eyes was wonderful. Sometimes, on coming in from our walk, I would sit down in my study chair and say quite casually, and in the ordinary tone of voice, "I wonder what they've done with my slippers?" He would then search all over the house for first one slipper and then the other. I would also say sometimes, "I wonder who has left that back door open? I wish you would kindly go down and shut it." Off he would rush, and, on his hind legs, bang the door until he shut it.

A cat and an African parrot I once had also developed the most extraordinary intelligence under the same system.

No canto porque me escuchen
Ni tampoes por que sé,
Canto porque soy mandado
Y es prenso obedecer.

(I sing, not that others may listen,
Nor because I know how ;
I sing because I am bidden,
And must needs obey.)

But *what* was he singing?

I do not know what this particular man was singing. I did not, although I should like to have done so, overtake him, present a phonograph at his head, and, *à la* José Maria,[1] command him to sing into it.

For this would have been the only way to reproduce the song for English hearers. I have, however, been able to bag the following specimens of *coplas*, taken down from the lips of muleteers,

---

[1] A famous brigand of these Sierras. I have seen a MS. left by the late Mr. Suter, who was for many years Consul at Xerez, in which he describes an adventure with this José Maria in the year 1832.

who constantly traverse the very spot, and have good-naturedly confessed what they had been singing. The English reader must not coldly criticise them, as if pen and paper had been taken in hand and they had been deliberately produced and fashioned. They are simply the improvised expressions of the untutored native of the wild Serrania.

As to the airs to which these *coplas* are sung, it is very difficult to express them in guitar tablature, or, for the matter of that, in any tablature. For the wild surroundings of which they are born are wanting. Moreover, it is impossible to fix the peculiar long drawn out *abandon* of some of the notes. As to singing them, I have tried hard to do so in the Sierras, but could not succeed —had not the heart for it, I suppose.

While in a lady's drawing-room, or, indeed, within the four walls of a house, I would as soon think of playing the Scotch bagpipes as attempt to render them.

With this reservation, the two following *Malagueñas* (the one *abandolada*, or forlorn; the other *trinada*, or trilled), very popular in this Serrania, are given as specimens. They have been very kindly committed to paper for me by a Spanish friend in Medina Sidonia, a clever player on the guitar, and the attempted explanations of the manner of rendering them are in substance his and not mine. So that the English reader may rest assured that he has put before him—I believe, after diligent inquiry, for the first time in English—genuine specimens, not only of native improvised *coplas*, but also of the airs to which they are sung.

MALAGUEÑA ABANDOLADO (*Forlorn*).

FOR STRINGED INSTRUMENTS.

This Malagueña, together with the one which follows, is played so as to alternate the tune with each one of the variations, in their order, or as may be desired.

PASEO (*measure*).

VARIACIONES.

THE SPANISH SIERRAS.

Here follows the accompaniment, to be taken while the person sings.

Each measure of the accompaniment to be repeated, as often as necessary; not fixedly, but the repetition to be made with a faster or slower movement, dependent on the time taken by the person singing, as he intones each verse or line of the verse.

The change, therefore, from the 1st to the 2nd, 3rd, or 4th of the tune in the accompaniment is made when it is remarked that the change of tone of each verse renders it necessary. The player has to have a very sharp ear to change opportunely.

MALAGUEÑA TRINADA (*Trilled*).

152 THE HEART AND SONGS OF

THE SPANISH SIERRAS.

Here follows the accompaniment, to be played while the person sings.

THE SPANISH SIERRAS.

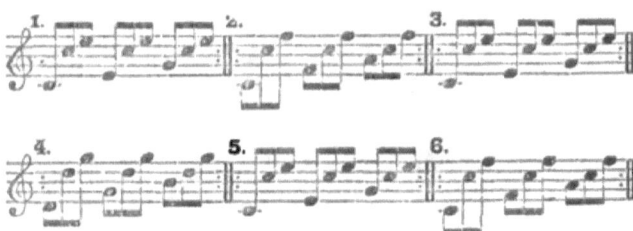

Each number of the accompaniment, &c., &c. **The same explanation** holds good here as in the former malagueña.

As is deduced from the explanation at the **beginning** of the other malagueña, they are both played thus:—The **tune is** played once, repeating its measures; then a variation, whichever may be desired, or in the order marked. Then the tune again; after this, a variation again. In a word, the tune must always be played before a variation.

THE HEART AND SONGS OF

COPLAS, TAKEN DOWN FROM THE LIPS OF MULETEERS AND PEASANTS IN THE SERRANIA.

When I pass along your street
I buy bread and go munching along,
Lest your mother should say
I am nourished by seeing you.

The grace of loving
Is neither bought nor inherited;
For 'tis God who gives it,
And you be left without.

When we knock at a door
And no voice replies,
It is a sign that in that house
They are very rich or very poor.

She doesn't love me because I'm old,
Your mother keeps on saying.
Let her go and ask the cabbages,
If old bacon be not good.

En el hoyo de tu barba
Dicen que me han de enterrar;
Que fortuna dueño mio
Quien se hubiera muerto ya.

---

[1] The above is a literal translation of the *coplas* in the Malagueña.

(In the dimple of your chin
They say that I'll be buried;
What bliss, my own
Were I dead already!)

Anda ve y díle á tu madre
Que te meta en un nichito,
Y te encienda cuatro velas,
Que yo no to necesito.

(Go and tell your mother
To put you in a little niche,
And light before you four candles
For I don't want you.)

De que le sirve al cantivo
Tener los grillos de plata
Y las cadenas de oro
Si la libertad le falta.

(What matters it to the captive
That his manacles are of silver,
And his chains of gold,
If he wants his liberty?)

Yo puse sitio a una plaza
Tan solo con un cañon;
Y a las veinte y cuatro horas
La plaza se un rindió.

(I laid siege to a stronghold
With one cannon only.
In four-and-twenty hours
The place surrendered to me.[1])

Tengo un vestido guardado
Que tiene cuatro colores
La ilusion y la esperanza
Los celos y los amores.

(I have a garment laid by
Which contains four colours—
Illusion, Hope
Jealousy, and Love.)

Dicen que me quieres dar
Soliman en la comida ;
En veniendo de tu mano
Soliman me dá la vida.

(They say you'd like to give me
Corrosive sublimate in my food ;
Coming from *thy* hand
Even poison would give life to me.

Desde aqui te estoy mirando
Y tu mirandome estas
Con los ojos *pillo, pillo,*
Pero no me pillaras.

---

[1] This would be sung by the *majo,* the dandy of the village.

(From here I gaze on thee
And thou on me
With eyes catchy ! catchy !
But you won't catch me.)

Dicen que tus ojos son
Dulces como el caramelo
Y yo como soy goloso
Por tus ojillos me muero.

(They say your eyes
Are sweet as caramel;
I am so fond of dainties
I would feed on your little eyes till I died.)

Dicen que los celos matan
Yo digo que no es asi ;
Que si los celos mataran
Me hubieran matado á mi.

(They say that jealousy kills,
I say it is not so;
Did jealousy kill
It would have killed me long ago.)

No hay quien me compre, Señores,
Una camisa sin mangas,
Sin delantero sin cuello,
Y sin lienzo en las espaldas.

(There is no one, gentlemen,
To buy of me a shirt without sleeves
Without front or collar,
And without a piece on the back.)

Cuentale al mundo tus dichas
Y no le cuentes tus penas
Que mas vale que te envidien
Que no que te compadezcan.

(Tell the world thy joys
But tell it not thy sorrows;
For it is better to be envied
Than it is to be pitied.)

Mas fatigas pasa un hombre
Cuando se vé despreciado
Que un *Chuzqué* cuando le amarran
Un chocolatero al rabo.

(Greater grief has a man
When he is contemned
Than a *Chuzqué*
With a chocolate pot tied to his tail.)

Yo me arrimé a un pedrégá
Por ver si me consolaba
Que aquel que tiene fatigas
Hasta con las piedras fabla.

(I approached a heap of stones,
Seeking to find some comfort,
For he that suffers grief
Will speak even to stones.)

San Juan y la Magdalena
Jugaban al esconder
San Juan le tiro un zapato
Por que no jugaba bien.

(St. John and the Magdalen
Were playing hide and seek,
St. John threw a shoe at her
Because she didn't play properly.)

Fatigas pasa una pulga
Cuando se ve entre los dedos
Mas fatigas paso yo
El dia que no te veo.

(Anxiety besets a flea
When he finds himself between the fingers.
Yet greater is my anxiety
When I don't see you for a whole day.)

El dia que tu nacistes
Callo un pedazo de cielo
Cuando te mueras y subas
Le tapara el agujero.

(The day you were born
A piece of heaven fell;
When you die and ascend
The gap will be filled up.)

Si mis ojos no te dicen
Todo lo que el pecho siente
No es por que se estan callados
Es por que no los comprendes.

(If my eyes don't tell you
All my bosom feels,
It is not because they are silent,
But because you do not understand.)

En un calabozo oscuro
Sufro penas sobre penas
Y a fuerza di estar a oscuras
Se ha vuelto mi pena negra.

(In a dungeon darksome
I suffer sorrow upon sorrow,
And from being so in the gloom
My sorrow has become black.)

Yo pedi lecencia a Dios
Que me dejare quererte,
Y Dios al ver mis fatigas
Me la otorgo para siempre.

(I prayed God for leave
To love thee,
And God, seeing my yearnings,
Granted my request for ever.)

Cuando el reloj dá las horas
Dice a todos sin reparo;
Al rico que ande deprisa;
Al pobre que ande desparcio.

(When the clock strikes the hours
It speaks to all impartially.
It says to the rich—go quickly,
To the poor—go slowly.)

El arbol de la esperanza
Solo dá frutos amargos;
Sus ojos son ilusiones
Sus flores son desengaños.

(The tree of Hope
Yields only bitter fruit.
Its leaves are illusions,
Its blossoms disillusions.)

Cinco sentidos tenernos
Todos los necesitamos;
Todos cinco los perdemos
Cuando nos enamoramos.

(We have five senses,
And we need them all;
We lose them all five
When we fall in love.)

Aunque eres angel, no quiero
Que me vengas a cantar
Que me hace muy poca gracia
La musica celestial.

(Although you are an angel
I don't want you to sing to me,
For celestial music
Has no *gracia* for me.)

En lo profundo del mar
Hay un castillo encantado;
En el que no entran mujeres
Para que dure el encanto.

(In the depths of the sea
There is an enchanted castle,
Into which no woman enters,
Lest the spell be broken.)

En verdad, dos son las cosas
Que el mundo entero gobiernan,
El oro, por lo que vale
Y el amor, por lo que cuesta.

(In truth there are two things
Which govern the whole world—
Gold, for what it is worth,
And love, for what it costs.)

Mi madre, mi pobre madre
Me digo mas de una vez,
" No basta que no hagas mal
Es preciso que hagas bien."

(My mother, my poor mother,
Told me more than once,
" It is not sufficient to do no ill,
It is needful to do good.")

Bastante castigo tiene
El que se quiere á si propio
Con no saber lo que vale
El querer bien a los otros.

(Punishment enough has he
Who loves himself alone,
In not knowing the worth
Of loving others.)

No te enorgullezcas tante
Dice la oja a la flor
Que de la misma semilla
Hemos nacido los dos.

("Don't grow so proud,"
Said the leaf to the flower,
"From the same seed
We both sprang.")

El amor que el egoista
Tiene a su propia persona
Es como el humo del fuego
Que no calienta y ahoga.

(The love which the egotist
Bears to his own person
Is like the smoke of fire
Which warms not, but stifles.

La mentira corre tante
Por atcanrar la verdad
Que en el impulso que lleva
Siempre se la deja atras.

(Falsehood runs so swiftly
To overtake the truth
That the impulse it carries
Always leaves it behind.)

Es triste, pero es seguro
Que de los pesares viejos
Ni uno seguiera se marcha
Mentras no llega otro nuevo.

('Tis no less sad than true,
That of old griefs
Not one departs
Whilst other new ones come.)

El hombre para ser hombre
Ha de tener tres partidas
Hacer mucho y habler poco
Y no alabarse en su vida.

(A man to be a man
Must have three accomplishments—
Must act much, speak little,
And never glorify himself.)

Tengo que hacer en el mundo
Una cosa sin ejemplo—
Te tengo que dar mi alma
Para completar tu cuerpo.

(I have to do in the world
One thing without example—
I must give you my soul
To complete your body.)

Una muger dio un chillido
Cuando salio el primer toro ;
Pensó que era su marido.

(A woman gave a shriek
When she saw the first bull enter;
She thought it was her husband.)

Dios te dé muy buenas noches
Hermosisima deidad
Encanto del universo
Prenda de la honestidad
Dios to dé muy buenas noches.

(God give thee a good night,
Most beauteous Deity,
Charm of the universe,
Gift of chastity,
God give thee a fair night.)

Si te se apaga el cigarro
No lo vuelvas a encender
Y amores que has olvidado
No los vuelvas a querer
Si te se apaga el cigarro.

(If your cigar goes out
Don't light it again.
The loves you have forgotten
Don't seek them again—
If your cigar goes out.)

El dia que tu naciste
Nacuron todas las flores
Y por ello te purveron
Maria de los Dolores.

(The day you were born
All the flowers sprang up;
For that reason they call thee
Maria de los Dolores [Griefs].)

Se sequen mis ojos
Si te miso chiquita del alma
Con malos antojos.

(May my eyes be dried up
If I look on you, little darling of my soul,
With evil longings.)

As regards set songs, I can only say that the well-known song of the Spanish Muleteer is totally unlike anything I ever heard. The following, rather, is a very good example of their style and manner, always premising that the *Rasqueádo* cannot be written down.

EL CABALLO O SOLO DE EL CONTRABANDISTA.

176   THE HEART AND SONGS OF

THE SPANISH SIERRAS.

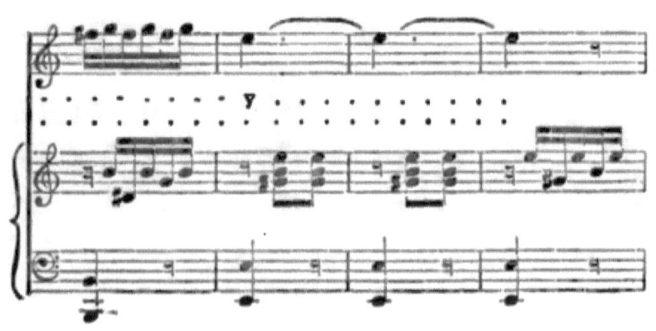

SECOND COPLA.

Faitigas y mas faitigas
Paso ausente de mi cielo
Y ella entretanto quien sabe
Se me fara gatupexio.

Ay Jaleo Jaleo
Muchacha,
&c.

THIRD COPLA.

Cuando debea a mi muchacha
Tendré el gusto y el consuelo
Que es una linda jitana
A quien con gracia camelo.

Ay Jaleo Jaleo
Muchacha,
&c.

Let me see—where were we? Oh! on the way from Ronda to Benoacaz, which now comes into view, nestling there in the distant valley, gleaming white as ever in this smokeless land. The charm compass had proved very useful since leaving Ronda, but now, having sighted the next halting-place, and the sun being very hot, dismounted and rested for awhile at a natural grotto containing a deep pool of water, pure as crystal, and adorned with maiden-hair and other ferns in rich luxuriance. The coolness, in contrast with the heat without, was delightful. Felt inclined to lie down, dream of Eden, and make for Benoacaz *mañana*.

. . . . .

O my learned Professor Teufelsdröckh, with thy fat belly and German pipe (I am sure thou hadst both), and thy "extensive, close-printed, close-meditated volume upon " Clothes ; their Origin and Influence " ! Like our friend Horace, neither wast thou a native of these Sierras of decent

Spain. Let me tell you that a *caballero*—his own policeman, caterer, and valet—on a journey like this, feels (and it is a novel, delightful feeling) that he is *not* "a botched mass of tailor's and cobbler's shreds," but "a tightly-articulated, homogeneous little figure, automatic, nay alive."

After washing face and hands in the crystal stream, and rinsing out Noblé's mouth, saddled, and up and off once more. Upon arrival at Benoacaz, completed my toilet with a shave in masterly style by a neat-handed little *barbero*.

The approach to Cortes, the next halting-place, would be very dangerous for one nervously inclined. At about a league from the village, upon rounding a bend in the mountain, came suddenly upon a particularly wild spot. At an immense depth beneath meandered a river through the tangled and broken valley, on the other side of which, to a still greater height than on this side, rose the purple Sierra—home of the keen-eyed vulture. Here there faced the traveller another mortuary cross—a human note truly, in weird harmony, upon the scored page of Nature. It was a safe spot for a deed of violence. Dismounting from old Noblé, I put my arm through the bridle-rein, and, while he ate the grass, copied the inscription, which was as follows :—

"AQUI MATARON
AD FRANCISCO
GARSIA SANCHEZ
DE EDAD DE 19 ANOS
E ANO DE 1848. SUS
PADRES Y HERMANOS
CONSERBAN

THE TAURO-MACHIAN SCHOOL, SEVILLE.

ESTA GRAN
MEMORIA.
 R. D."

(Here they killed
AD Francisco
Garsia Sanchez,
Aged 19 years,
In the year 1848. His
parents and brothers
preserve
this great
memorial.)

This murder or "taking off," whichever it may have been, it will be observed, took place in the same year as the last, namely, 1848. This was only a year or two after the Civil Guards were instituted. Perhaps these men were robbers whom the Civil Guard, after a prayer said for their souls, shot there and then. Or it may have been that this young man, aged 19, was killed by the other, Mimoantoni, who was afterwards himself captured by the Guard and slain. Or, perhaps, these men met their deaths in sudden quarrel—the hot blood stirred, knives snatched from the *fajas*,[1] and one or both of the erewhile friends, may be, left weltering in their blood. But whatever it may have been, of one thing I feel sure, that neither of them fell a victim to Revenge. For the Spaniard is not revengeful. Anything like the cruel and un-Christian *vendetta* is unknown. Thus at the *Fiesta de Toros*, at carnival time, or in moments of excitement, the attention is perhaps

---

[1] Every Spaniard carries a knife in his *faja*, or sash round the loins. These knives are of two kinds. There is the ordinary Spanish clasp knife, like the one I carried myself wherewith to *comer*. And there is the murderous *navaja de muelle*, or clasp knife with a spring, so that when once opened it cannot be shut. This latter, I believe, the Civil Guards may now take away from anybody.

drawn to a commotion going on. Two are at each other with knives. A *guardia*, if handy, or friends, if they can manage it skilfully, separate them, and all is soon forgotten : no animosity remains. I remember once, during the carnival in Xerez being much amused. Two men suddenly drew their knives. It happened to be near a lamp-post. A bystander adroitly linked his arm into the disengaged arm of one of them, and walked with him backwards round and round the lamp-post until he evidently was unable to tell at which point of the compass his adversary was, and, although before white with passion, it was all over in a moment. In fact, I fancy, from observation of the behaviour of spectators, that Spaniards actually sympathise with each other on their liability to these outbreaks of passion.

The first thing that catches the eye upon nearing Cortes is the white tower of the church. It was in this village that I made the acquaintance of a charming, sympathetic, warm-hearted peasant woman, the mother of five young children—four girls and a baby boy in the cradle. The eldest of the girls —a bright, sweet, intelligent child of about eight summers, with limbs as lithe and supple as a chamois, her bonny black hair confined by a gay *panuela* — was knitting (but not demurely) while the mother rocked the cradle and sang to her latest born a simple ditty, the air being much like that given below. It was a pretty picture of peace, coming just after the contemplation of those tragic records outside in the wild Serrania. I ventured to make her acquaintance by looking in and asking the way to the *Correo*. In the course of conversation, full of self-respect, and yet so *sympatico* and womanly, she alluded to the *consumos* and the way the people were taxed. Even the fish they catch for themselves, she said, was so taxed that it did not help a family to eke out a slender living.

CRADLE SONGS.

Niño chiquirritito
De pecho y cuna,
¿ Dónde estará tu madre
Que no te arrulla?

(Tiny little one
Of the bosom and cradle,
Where can your mother be
That she does not sing to thee?)

Señora Santa Ana,
Señor San Joachin,
Arrulad al niño
Que quiere dormir.

(Señora Saint Anne,
Señor Saint Joachim,
Sing to the child
Who wants to sleep.)

A la puerta del cielo
Venden zapatos
Para los angelitos,
Que están descalzos.

(At the gate of heaven,
They sell little shoes
For the little angels,
Who are barefooted.)

A los niños que duermen
Dios los bendice,
Y á las madres que velan
Dios las asiste.

(Children who go to sleep,
God blesses them;
And mothers who watch,
God helps them.)

Corazoncito mio
Calla y no llores,
Que te traigo noticia
De tus amores.

(Child of my heart,
Be quiet and don't cry,
For I bring you news
Of your loves.)

Anda véte, morito,
A la moreria
Que mi niño no entiende
Tu algarabia.

(Go away, little Moor,
To the Moorish quarter,
For my boy doesn't understand
Your gibberish.)

Up with the lark in the morning and off for Algar. Soon after starting the rain came down in torrents, so took refuge in a *venta* and tucked into a tremendous breakfast of *huevos y cochino*, feeling all the time that I was doing my duty as an Englishman. About two o'clock the rain ceased for a time. If Algar was now to be reached before nightfall it was evident that no time was to be lost, so pushed on with all speed. But the night did creep on, and the rains descended, and the floods came. The track became less and less distinguishable and was at length lost. Pushed on, however, trusting now more to Noblé's instinct than anything else. As it turned out afterwards, his instinct led him in the right direction. But a horror of thick darkness was now coming on apace, and it seemed likely to be a case of spending the night in the open—wet through and shivering. What is that? A flickering light.

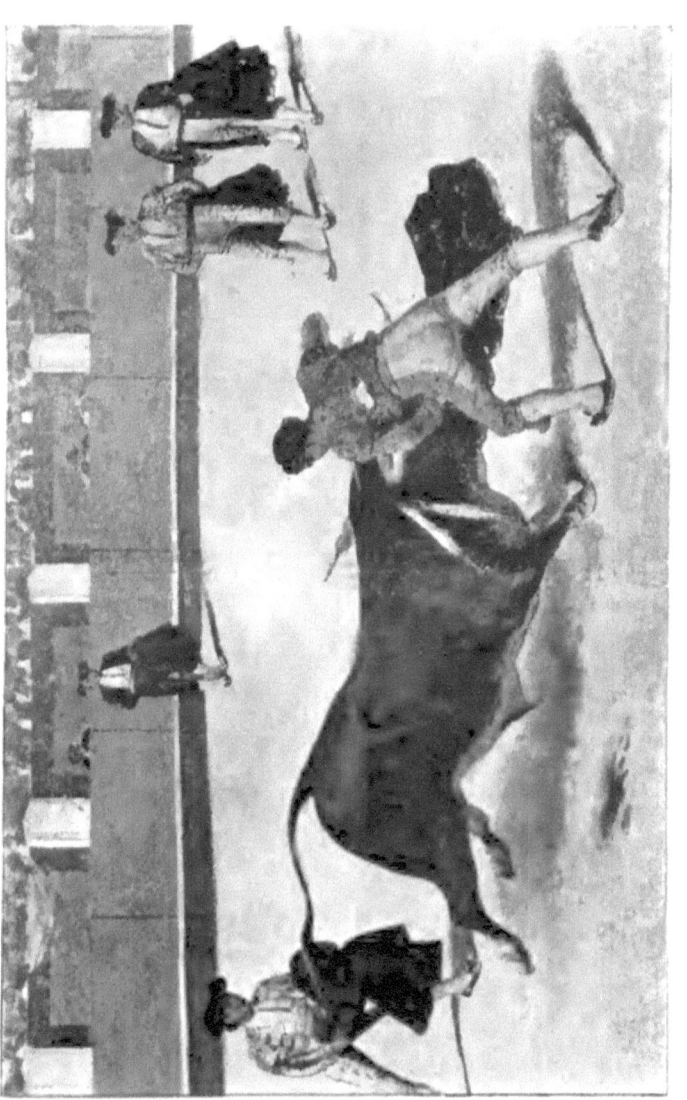

THE HERO OF THE DAY.

Made towards it, and found it to proceed from a wretched little *ventorillo*, in which a man was sitting over a burning *brasero*, two others being in shadow. I did not like the look of the place at all, but there was no help for it, so riding up to the entrance, I asked, "*Donde es el camina para Algar?*" The man at the *brasero* came out, peered into my face, laid his left hand on my bridle-rein, and said, curtly, "*Qué?*" It was a cut-throat, villainous face, and as the action itself was suspicious, and his right hand at liberty to slip out his *navaja*, I thought it best to grasp my revolver firmly, and, without actually presenting it at his head, let him see that I was prepared to defend myself. I then repeated my question in as menacing a tone as his own. The two men in the shadow said something to him. He let go the bridle, and said that Algar was about a league to the right. I thought this was possibly a trap, but there was nothing else to do but to follow the direction. Moving on as noiselessly as possible, with hand grasping the revolver in case of a surprise, it was an immense relief at length to see in the distance the gleam as of a candle. Found it to proceed from a sort of *venta*. The people here were so curt and sullen that the thought occurred to me that possibly they were in league with those rascals at the *ventorillo*. Permission was given with a very ill grace to stay there until the morning. To sleep in wet clothes upon a mattress flung down upon the bare earth did not look very promising. Although thoroughly exhausted, could only sleep with one eye open, and that fixed upon the door, which was unlocked.

Departed with the morning light for Arcos and home. At Arcos had a dry, a shave, and a wash-up. Looked my tried friend and companion Noblé over too, in order to return him safe and sound to his owner, Walter Buck, Esq., of Xerez, at whose hospitable mansion we arrived just as the sun had sunk to rest.

THE END.

The Gresham Press,
UNWIN BROTHERS,
CHILWORTH AND LONDON.

www.ingramcontent.com/pod-product-compliance
Lightning Source LLC
Chambersburg PA
CBHW032229230426
43666CB00033B/1649